# Tosh

*An amazing true story of life,
death, danger and drama in the
Garda Sub-Aqua Unit*

TOSH LAVERY
WITH
GERARD CROMWELL

PENGUIN
IRELAND

PENGUIN IRELAND

UK | USA | Canada | Ireland | Australia
India | New Zealand |South Africa

Penguin Ireland is part of the Penguin Random House group of companies
whose addresses can be found at global.penguinrandomhouse.com.

First published 2015
001

Copyright © Tosh Lavery, 2015

The moral right of the author has been asserted

Set in 13.5/16 pt Garamond MT Std
Typeset by Jouve (UK), Milton Keynes
Printed in Great Britain by Clays Ltd, St Ives plc

A CIP catalogue record for this book is available from the British Library

ISBN: 978–1–844–88358–5

www.greenpenguin.co.uk

For Susan, Thomas and Philip

# Contents

# CONTENTS

# Preface

If you can swim, you would probably jump into a swimming pool without much hesitation. But if you were told that there were three dead people somewhere under the water, would you still jump in? What if the lights were switched off and the pool was in darkness?

Diving to recover the body of somebody who has drowned or been murdered is a sombre undertaking and not for everybody. There are places where you can learn how to search for a knife or a gun, but no training centre in the world has dead bodies waiting for you at the bottom of a pool. There is nothing that will prepare you for finding the dead.

If you go out to Kilkee or somewhere for a weekend of diving with your friends, and you have a few drinks the night before and wake up with a hangover, you don't have to get into the water. But if you are a garda diver and you get the call to search for a missing person, it doesn't matter how hung-over you are. It doesn't matter what you're at, be it a first communion, a wedding or a funeral. It doesn't matter where you're supposed to be with your family. It doesn't matter how sick you are. You're getting in.

Apart from the grieving family of whoever you are searching for, there could be maybe 300 onlookers standing on a river bank waiting for you to do your job, sometimes even television cameras and photographers' lenses bearing down on you. It's then that the loudmouths go quiet. It's then that the reality of the situation kicks in.

You can't help being afraid every time you stick your head into the water and enter that eerily quiet world under the surface. In good visibility you can try to carry out a systematic search, but in bad conditions there is only one way to locate anything. By touch. You crawl along the bottom and literally feel your way around, not knowing what you're going to find.

In over thirty years as a garda diver, I saw the bodies of fishermen lost at sea in some of Ireland's biggest maritime disasters. The bodies of children pulled from the icy depths. Murder victims, some hacked into pieces and packed into shopping bags. Suicides. I've seen them all and, more often than not, pulled them out myself.

I've often heard guys boast about how they were never scared or worried about the upcoming dive. They're liars. They are the ones to watch, the ones who are all talk at the bar the night before after a few drinks.

The morning after, when it's cold and wet and you're putting on all the gear, pulling your mask over your face and sticking the regulator in your mouth as you get ready to dive into a dirty, muddy lake in poor visibility, it's always a different story.

# I

# Water baby

My father, Philip Lavery, was seventeen years older than my mother, Margaret Shanahan, when they met at a dance in Hourigan's Hall near the village of Doon, County Limerick, in 1943. Having cycled the fifteen miles from his home in Herbertstown, County Limerick, and danced with young Margaret that night, my father plucked up the courage to ask her out and the customary courting, engagement and wedding duly followed. They were married in St Michael's Church in Tipperary town in June 1946. As her father had passed away, a friend of the family, Garda John Murphy, walked my mother up the aisle.

Afterwards, the newlyweds cycled the thirty-five miles to Nenagh on their High Nelly bikes for their honeymoon, to stay with a cousin in Portroe. Halfway there, they stopped for a picnic at a milk stand, a roadside halt where the local farmer would leave his churns of milk to be collected by the dairy truck. When they got to Portroe, my mother realized she had left her purse on the milk stand and my father had to cycle back to get it. He retrieved the purse and arrived back to Nenagh later that evening – her knight in shining armour.

Just ten months later, in April 1947, their firstborn child,

Eileen, arrived. She was followed by another girl, Maureen, and their firstborn son, Myles, before I came along on 7 August 1953. Despite being sandwiched in between those three and my younger brothers Philip and Noel, I somehow grew to become the apple of my mother's eye.

Having moved to Waterford to work as a farm steward after they got married, my father looked after cattle for Lord Lionel Richardson on his large estate on the edge of town (next to where Kilcohan Park greyhound stadium now lies), where, my mother told me later, His Lordship could often be heard bellowing for 'Lavery' to come and attend calving or some other duty in the early hours of the morning, even on Christmas Day. My formative years were spent in a cramped little lodge at the end of the avenue leading up to Lord Richardson's manor. I don't remember much about it, apart from the swirls of butter and the odd egg my mother used to bring home from her job in the dairy there.

With five children already in the little lodge, Lord Richardson warned my parents that if they had any more they would have to leave, so when my mother fell pregnant for the sixth time they had a problem. They confided in the local priest, Father Pat Power, who helped them apply for a council house just down the road and also found my father a new job in the Clover Meats factory in town. My parents planned their move without telling Lord Richardson and when they eventually got the council house they loaded all their stuff onto the back of local coalman Maurice Foley's truck in the dead of night and we left without trace.

I was only about five years old then but I can remember the move to Waterford's Pearse Park housing estate well. The 'new' bungalow in Pearse Park was almost derelict when we arrived and we had to wade through about five feet of grass to get in the door. Inside, the floors were bare and I remember the echoes as we entered the sitting room, where a scorched bicycle tyre sat proudly in the fireplace.

Although it was bigger than the lodge at Richardson's, it was tiny by today's standards. There were three bedrooms: a box room not big enough to swing a cat, where my two sisters slept, another bedroom where us four boys slept, two to a bed, and a back bedroom for my parents. I can even remember us four brothers sharing the same bed at one point; two at the top and two at the bottom, with old army coats draped over us to keep us warm in the winter.

Even though the house was small and us kids were constantly growing and taking up more space as we did so, a room was always made available for the guard who had given my mother away and he used to come and stay with us for the horse races in Tramore every year.

Bit by bit, the house was tidied up and decorated and by the time my father had finished with the garden we had our own vegetables growing out the back. When we were young, he'd have us pulling the onions and carrots, cleaning them off and putting them on the roof of the shed to dry off before selling them to the local vegetable shop.

My mother had always worked hard, and after a while she bought an old NSU scooter to get her to a new waitressing job in the Grand Hotel in Tramore. She would travel the seven miles in time for the breakfast serving, come back home to stick some bread or apple tarts in the oven and then head back again for the lunch sitting. Often she'd come home again and give us something to eat as we got in from school and then return for the tea service if the hotel was busy. She was always on the go and, as a devout teetotaller, wore a shiny Pioneer badge pinned to her uniform every day.

Directly across the road from our house stood a convent school where my siblings and I started school until a new primary school, Scoil Lorcáin, was built in the neighbouring St John's Park estate. After finishing in Scoil Lorcáin, I went on to the Christian Brothers at Mount Sion. Although I didn't particularly like school, I never mitched or skipped classes for fear my father would find out and I'd get a clatter. My father didn't take too kindly to cheeky or rebellious behaviour. I remember one day clipping one of the Christian Brothers' robes with my foot as we stood in the school line and being sent home, where I spent most of the afternoon hiding down the bottom of the garden waiting for my father to come home to give me a beating, but in the end my mother protected me from him and I got off lightly.

But my father wasn't the only one to be feared, with our not-so-Christian Brother teachers quickly earning a reputation for brutality. I found myself on the receiving end of a beating one day when the local bread man pulled up outside our house during lunch break. As usual, I sauntered over and looked in at the mouth-watering array of cakes and buns on the various pull-out trays in the back of the bread van.

When I pulled out one of the trays for a closer inspection it collapsed and everything landed on the ground. The bread man went into the school and reported the incident to the Christian Brother we had nicknamed 'Birdy' for his short stocky stature and Robin redbreast style of walking. He was also renowned for carrying a thick leather strap in his breast pocket. That day he dragged me into the class and, in front of all my classmates, viciously beat me across the arms, upper body and head with the strap. 'Birdy' was clever enough not to leave marks where my parents could see them, though, so I said nothing when I went home for fear of getting another beating off them for getting into 'trouble' in school.

School holidays were spent playing soccer on the road or swimming in anything that was deep enough. But both activities came with a set of problems. The main concern when playing football on the road was being caught by the local garda sergeant and getting fined. Even though there wasn't much traffic at the time, it was an offence to play football on the road and, laughable as it may seem nowadays, plenty of my friends were summonsed to appear in court and fined ten shillings for doing so. Providing the match ball for these games put you in a predicament. If you didn't put your name on the ball it would most likely be robbed by the end of the game, but if you did and the sergeant found it, you would lose the ball anyway and also be the one who got fined. A lot of League of Ireland players came from our road and many of them – including former Waterford United stars Tony Dunphy and my brother Noel – acquired their speed by scattering over walls, garden fences and into ditches at the sight of Sergeant Gleeson approaching on his bike.

Kilcohan Park stadium was just up the road, with a soccer pitch inside the greyhound track, and match day would see us sneak in under the tin fence to watch the all-conquering Waterford United team in action. If a steward or a garda saw us, they'd chase us as the crowd roared us on before allowing us to disappear into their midst and escape.

Although we only lived a few miles away from the beach, a trip to the seaside was a rare and special treat for us as youngsters. I remember being brought to the beach in Tramore on the back of my mother's bicycle as a very young child while my father rode beside us with my brother on his crossbar and my sister on the back carrier. On the rare occasion that the whole family went to Tramore on the train, my parents would pay for two kids and send the rest of us in under the barriers. Once on board the train, they'd send us down a few carriages and if a ticket inspector asked for tickets, we'd vaguely point behind us and say our parents had them 'down there somewhere'. With the pram filled with sandwiches, we'd have a family picnic and spend the day playing in the sand and paddling in the water.

Neither of my parents could swim a stroke but they sometimes ventured out into the little waves lapping up onto the sand, my father up to his ankles and my mother maybe up to her waist. I remember an adult from the area, Alex Stubbs, drowning during one of those early beach trips with my family. He was brought in out of the sea by a lifeguard wearing a white hat, who in turn was on the end of a reel of rope being pulled towards the beach by others. But I was so young that the dangers of the water were lost on me back then.

By the time I was about nine I was messing about in water up to my waist and, after a spell of trial and error, was able to swim underwater for short periods. A real water baby, I had no fear and, once I could move in it, I was soon venturing into deeper water. The best place to swim back then was in a local lake owned by another landlord, a Major Carew. To get to the major's you had to walk about four miles across roads and through cornfields, and every summer, groups of kids brandishing towels – and togs, if they could afford them – regularly got into trouble with the local farmer for traipsing pathways through his corn on the way to the lake. On a sunny day there could be forty kids at the lake, with us Pearse Park kids often squaring off against 'the Johnnies' – the kids from St John's Park estate – for swimming and diving rights.

As a nine-year-old, the lake seemed as big as Loch Ness but in reality it was no more than the size of a Gaelic football pitch, with a small island in the middle where a lone tree took pride of place. While the smooth water's surface was punctured by weeds around most of the lake, there was a twenty-feet-wide pathway in the water cleared by days of kids swimming across to the island. As I couldn't yet swim on the surface, I simply dived in and swam underwater until I could feel the grassy banks on the other side.

Major Carew employed a land steward to watch over his property but he rarely paid any attention to us kids, unless we were on one of our military-style raids of his orchard or glasshouses for apples or peaches. I got walloped from my mother upon my return from one of these raids with a jumper full of apples. She wasn't unduly worried about where I'd got the apples; she was more concerned that I'd pulled my brand-new jumper out of shape.

When CIÉ dug up the old railway line from Tramore to Waterford in 1961, it left a deep trench in the bog, about fifteen feet wide, running parallel to the main road for a few miles. That trench soon became our outdoor swimming pool. Here, we'd swim naked as the passengers on the bus to Tramore looked down – I can imagine what they were thinking about the grubby little urchins below.

Like at the major's, there was a pecking order in the bog, and a deeper section called the 'big bend' a bit further down was where the bigger youths used to dive in and swim. To be 'allowed' down there by the older kids was a badge of honour and didn't come easy, but I was just about able to swim across the width of the bog and hadn't a clue how to tread water, so it took me a while to swim in the big bend.

Shortly after I had gone home one summer's day, a youngster dived into the same bog, got his head stuck in between two wooden poles under the water, possibly remnants of the old railway line, and drowned.

When I was about ten, I finally learned to swim properly on a visit to my brother's Scout camp in Courtown Harbour in Wexford. I went out into the water, where two brothers from Waterford, the Twomeys, held me up and showed me how to swim on the surface for the first time. After that, there was no stopping me.

I spent most of those childhood summers with my best friends Mick McGrath, Paul 'Dakar' Freeman and Denny Flynn, but some of the older teenagers from the area also strutted around the major's lake. Some of this gang wore leather belts outside their togs with knives stuffed into them like the popular TV hero of the time, Tarzan of the Jungle. I remember one of them even brandishing a hatchet one day too. They were older, bigger and tougher than my friends, and, while I wasn't afraid to stand my ground even at that age, I was always a bit wary of them.

As it turned out, I had every right to be. On the way home from training with the local Enterprise Boxing Club one evening in 1964, I walked past an alleyway to see the same lads throwing knives at a cat they had tied up. Not long after that, the guy with the hatchet, who was just fifteen at the time, had an altercation with another youth outside a dance hall on Mayor's Walk. Another member of the gang handed him a knife and he stuck it into the chest of another youngster, Jimmy Galvin, killing him. Afterwards, he threw the knife into the river Suir. It was the first murder in Waterford for twenty-five years. The guards found the culprit later that night. He was sitting on a wall about a mile away in Ferrybank, crying.

The only time I brandished a knife myself was when I decided to bring my father's butcher's knife with me to join my friends stealing turnips one night in a local field owned by a farmer called Farrell, whom we nicknamed 'the Bull'. Instead of just taking a few turnips, though, my friends and I pulled up piles of them and fired them across the road, with no thought for the farmer's livelihood or, indeed, my father's part-time job with him at the time. Somebody saw us, though, and I was brought home by the gardaí. My father told them that he would deal with me himself. I got a few clatters and never took his knife again.

By the time I'd gone into sixth class in national school, my friends and I could scrape together the few pence required to make our way out to Tramore on the bus and spend the day on the beach and swimming in the sea. On one of these trips, we heard a commotion a few hundred yards away and went down to see, laid out on the beach, the body of Bill Farrell, a kid from my class in Mount Sion who was one of my friends. As they pronounced him dead his younger brother, who was only six or seven at the time, took a half-crown out of Bill's pocket, turned to his friend and asked, 'Bill won't be needing that now, so he won't?' The little boy's innocence in that moment of tragedy has stayed with me always.

Although I now knew that the water was dangerous, those drownings didn't put me off. As my swimming got better, I began to look for the biggest and best places to jump in, progressing from edging out onto the outside branch of the tree over Major Carew's lake and diving into the water, to jumping off bridges and even cranes down on the docks in Waterford. When I was about thirteen, most of the older teens from the major's had graduated to diving in off the pier in Tramore and I used to sneak up and dive in off the storm wall with them. At the time, my mother and father didn't know where I was and if I'd gone under, they'd still be looking for me. I look at the pier now and it seems a midget of a thing but, back then, it was like diving off the cliffs of Acapulco and nothing would do me until I got up there. Once I was able to dive off the wall, swim around the pier, climb up the steps and jump back in, it wasn't long until I graduated to the Guillamene, a popular local swimming spot, like Dublin's Forty Foot.

With my father now working as a kennel man at the greyhound track in Kilcohan Park, I earned a few pence by minding parked cars on race nights. By fifteen, I had a little job walking the greyhounds out of trap two and also did odd jobs around the place, cutting the grass and white-washing the walls among other things. I got ten bob for walking the greyhounds but often won more by betting on tips from the owners or turning a blind eye to their efforts to manipulate the outcome of races – either boosting their dog's chances of winning by removing its muzzle or mak-ing sure a dog lost by giving it a handful of food as it was pushed into the trap.

Although I always put a few bob into a savings account every week, with money in my pocket from the track, trips to the beach to swim with Mick and Dakar were soon replaced by trips to dances at the weekends. Although they were still in school and, like me, were a couple of years shy of taking their Leaving Certificate, Mick and Dakar both started drinking, while I stayed away from it.

Territorial fights were ten-a-penny at these dances and it wasn't uncommon to be chased by an angry mob after being seen dancing with one of a rival gang's girls. With drink on him, Dakar began to get involved in fights with lads our age from the countryside. I tried to hold him up in the middle of a melee one night. We ended up running out of the place and being chased home towards Waterford, seven miles away.

Dakar's luck ran out one night, though, when he got involved in yet another ruckus at a dance. At fifteen years of age, he got arrested and was sentenced to two years in the reformatory school in Daingean, County Offaly. I travelled to Daingean with him and his parents in a car they had borrowed from his father's boss, who was the local undertaker. As Dakar got out, we stayed in the car and watched as a giant of a Christian Brother grabbed Dakar's case, put his hand on his shoulder and brought him inside, then closed the door behind him.

At the time, nobody realized what was going on behind those closed doors but it later came to light that a lot of the young lads held there were brutalized and even raped by members of the religious order that ran the school.

Some people say that it's the first drink rather than the last one that that kills an alcoholic and my first drink came when I was seventeen years old and heading to a dance with my older brother, Myles, and two of his friends. Of the four of us, I was the one with the money, from my job at the greyhound track, and the other three knew it, which is probably why I was invited to the 21 Bar, or Sexton's, in an area known as the Car Stand in Waterford. While the lads ordered large bottles of stout, I drank from a small bottle and, after buying three rounds, was feeling a bit googly eyed when I turned to an old man sitting at the counter beside me.

'Jaysus, I can't drink at all,' I said.

The old man turned to me and said something that I have never forgotten since.

'Son, the day will come when you won't be able to afford to get drunk.'

Like the swimming and diving, I progressed onto bigger things and was soon drawn into the same sort of fights and scrapes as the others.

One afternoon, while diving at the pier in Tramore, I was arrested, thrown into the back of a patrol car and driven to Tramore garda station by a detective. I had been seen talking to a local sixteen-year-old who, it turned out, was under surveillance for his involvement in a spate of burglaries in the area. When the detective finally realized that I'd literally just met the other guy while swimming, he let me go, but not before I made him give me a lift back down to the pier.

I had to appear in court twice as a teenager: once getting fined ten shillings for having a pillion passenger on my mother's little Honda 50 while holding a provisional licence and another time getting the Probation Act for fighting at a soccer match in Cork. Luckily the fighting incident never went on my record so it didn't go against me when I applied for jobs later on.

I don't know if it was my boxing background that earned me the reputation for being a bit of a scrapper, but one day while I was working at the greyhound track the manager, Paddy Grant, came up with a new way of making a few bob for myself and a workmate. Paddy owned a pub on Slieve Rua, just outside the town, and told us about a particular customer who came in and wrecked the place most nights, causing rows with customers and staff. He wanted to know if we'd be able to 'solve the problem' for him.

The two of us went to the bar one night, sat down, had a drink and waited. Sure enough, within minutes the problem customer arrived and announced himself to all by kicking the door in and roaring and shouting. We grabbed him, pulled him outside and, while the other fella did lookout, I gave him a few wallops. Then we both ran down the road. Minutes later, Paddy pulled up alongside us, gave us a lift home and an extra few bob for our trouble. Although we solved the problem for Paddy – the customer never came back – thug-for-hire wasn't a business I ever went into again.

My friends and I had found another pub in town, McLoughlins, that would serve us young lads in the back room, and from then on, even though I saved a few bob from the track in the post office every week, I always made sure to have money for four or five large bottles of stout every Friday evening and drinking became a regular part of my week.

In October 1970, the beginning of my Leaving Certificate year, I travelled to Dublin on the train for the meeting of Waterford United and Glasgow Celtic in the European Cup, the equivalent of today's Champions League. Having drunk the whole way up on the train, I got into such a state that I remember very little of the day, apart from my brother Philly having to carry me most of the way to Lansdowne Road, and stopping at O'Connell Bridge to vomit into the river Liffey.

When I got expelled from Saturday-morning art class for throwing a duster at another pupil, I found I could get served in another pub, Batterberry's, on Barrack Street, right next door to Mount Sion, and Friday evenings with the lads were followed by Saturday-morning visits for a shandy as a 'cure' before school. (We had a half-day on a Thursday and school on Saturday mornings.)

When Mick McGrath got a job and Denny Flynn moved to Scotland, I started hanging out with Nicky Power, John Doyle, Tony Gaffney and John Hennessy, all of whom were three or four years older than me. At seventeen, I thought I was great, drinking with all the older fellas. My parents never suspected a thing about my drinking, mainly because they'd be in bed asleep before I got home and, of course, they'd never dream of me drinking during school hours.

Despite the drinking and messing, I managed to get a decent Leaving Certificate and, having passed my exams in the summer of 1971, it was time to get a proper job. Waterford Crystal was the biggest employer in the area. My brother Myles and friends Mick and Dakar were all working in the glass factory so I tried for a job there too. The test to get in consisted of being put on a glass-cutting wheel and practising cutting on broken bits of glass before being asked to cut a star shape into a piece of good glass at the end of the day.

From the minute you went into the factory, a button was pressed and everybody's cutting wheel began to spin with water streaming down a little piece of leather on top of it to keep it cool. With health and safety unheard of at the time, all you could hear for the rest of the day was the high-pitched whine of these glass-cutting machines buzzing in your ears. I managed to fail the entrance test no fewer than three times: the star shape cut into my final piece of glass was always off.

So, for a year or so after the Leaving, I worked in temporary jobs. The most lucrative was one where I wandered through local fields laying cables for an exploration company hoping to mine the area. With money in my pocket I could keep drinking. Each Monday morning I'd always make sure I was up at seven so that I could go into the early house down the docks before I was collected for laying cables at eight. I only came to realize why the job was so lucrative one day when a farmer roared at me from across a field to warn me that he had lost cattle and donkeys in the bog I was walking across. After a few months, the mining company decided not to pursue their tests any further and I was unemployed again.

Six months after I had left school, at the beginning of 1972, I was preparing job applications to send to the bank and the army cadets. I was about to get photographs taken to send in with my applications when my mother told me that 1,000 new jobs were to be made available in An Garda Síochána and showed me an ad in the national paper looking for new recruits. To please my mother, I got an extra photo taken and applied for a job in the guards as well.

## 2

# Becoming one of O'Malley's Midgets

With the Troubles having started in Northern Ireland three years earlier, by 1972 more gardaí were needed along the border and, in an effort to encourage applications for training, recruiting restrictions were lifted or eased by Minister for Justice Desmond O'Malley. Recruits still had to be 'unmarried, of good character and in good health' but the lower age limit was reduced from nineteen to eighteen and the upper limit raised from twenty-five to twenty-six. If you had passed the Leaving Certificate with at least a D or pass mark in both English and Irish, you no longer had to sit the entrance exam. But it was the reduction in the minimum height requirement – from five feet nine inches to five feet eight – that the national media and the general public latched on to, ensuring that the new garda recruits that year became known as 'O'Malley's Midgets'.

My Leaving Cert results meant that I didn't have to do the entrance exam, so the first part of my application was to present myself at the local garda station, where Sergeant Mick Johnson checked that I had no convictions and measured me. At five feet eight and a half inches, I was tall enough – just – but my chest didn't meet the thirty-six-inch requirement. I spent about a month in the local park afterwards hanging out of trees, running and doing press-ups in an effort to build up my chest.

When I returned a month later to be measured again, I made the cut and, out of around forty Waterford applicants, I was the first to be sent for an interview in Dublin. Looking back, I wonder if a friend of my parents – a local guard whose wife worked in the hotel with my mother – might have pulled a few strings for me.

Having got through the interview, passed the medical (once I had complied with an instruction to have a wisdom tooth removed) and somehow avoided being summonsed when I was stopped for driving my mother's car without a licence (never heard another word about it – again, I later wondered whether someone had intervened on my behalf), I received a letter saying I'd been called into the guards.

At the same time, another arrived saying I had got the job I'd applied for in the bank. Without really thinking about it – perhaps because I knew my mother would be delighted – I chose the guards. I was told to report to Templemore Garda Training College on 5 July 1972, when I would commence eighteen weeks' training.

My mother went to Shaw's department store and bought me a huge hard-shell suitcase, a new pair of pyjamas and a silk dressing gown. When the day came to go to Templemore she was so happy to have a son joining the guards that she agreed to let me drive there. As I tore down through the middle of Waterford city, I met an oncoming van on a narrow section of road. Instead of pulling over and letting the van past, though, I drove him up onto the footpath and kept going. My mother – all dressed up beside me in the front passenger seat – didn't blink an eye. My father, suited and booted in the back, said nothing either, even when I flew round a sharp bend on the wrong side of the road later on.

We stopped at a pub in Cashel for lunch and for the first time ever I had a drink with my father. Apart from at Christmas, he rarely drank alcohol but he had a bottle of stout that day. I had a shandy. For the rest of the trip all I was worried about was whether they would be able to smell the drink off me in Templemore and send me home. My parents said goodbye at the gate and left me there as they weren't allowed in. After enrolling in the gymnasium, 150 of us, all male, stood in lines, put our hands up in the air and the biggest ever batch of recruits was sworn in as members of An Garda Síochána.

Nowadays, young guards in Templemore each have their own room, with a desk and a bed and wardrobe. Back then we were shown to a vast dormitory, split into partitions with three beds and three built-in wardrobes in each and with a three-foot gap between the ceiling and the top of each partition. The beds were metal framed, covered with old spring mattresses and dressed with heavy, itchy, grey woollen blankets. The toilets and showers were at the end of a long corridor.

The thing that impressed me most about the campus was the swimming pool. The only pool I had seen before was when my friends and I climbed in over the wall of Newtown Girls' School in Waterford one night, found the swimming-pool door open, pulled back the cover and sneakily swam in it. Upon being brought up to the viewing deck to look down on the garda pool, the first thing that came into my head was, *I'm going to jump in off here.*

With our tour over, we got a fry-up for our tea in the canteen, sat around and had a chat for a while before going to bed early in anticipation of our first day's training. For someone from a council house in Waterford, who had never been anywhere apart from Dublin Zoo for a day, to be suddenly living with fellas from all over the country was a totally new experience and a bit of a shock to the system.

After a breakfast of tea and toast the next morning, we went out onto the square at nine o'clock, where the sergeant, Pat Tierney, ordered us to line up with the 'shortest on the left, tallest on the right. Quick march!' It didn't take long for us to figure out that I should run to the left-hand end every morning and that a guy called Eddie Morgan, who was six feet three, should run to the right.

After some instructions and a few words about what we would be doing in Templemore, Sergeant Tierney inquired if there were any questions from his new recruits.

'Will we be getting paid weekly?' I asked.

'Yes, you will, and very weakly,' came the reply before Tierney looked down at my shoes and told me that it would be the last time I'd be wearing 'those brothel creepers' out in the yard. We were then sent to the store for our uniforms, where we were like kids at a fancy-dress party trying on our new boots, woollen trousers, shirts with a studded collar and tunics. Everyone also got a cap with their number on it as well as a baton, a whistle and a pair of handcuffs. A clean uniform and polished shoes were a necessity in Garda College, as were black socks and a tight haircut.

Pretty soon we got into a regular routine. Every morning, I'd hurry down the hall, looking like Muhammad Ali in my new silk dressing gown. (While most of us rushed to get a shower before the water went cold, some fellas simply never bothered with hygiene at all and there was an outbreak of scabies and head lice on one of the other dorms in my time there.) After that we ran over to the canteen for a bowl of cereal, toast and tea. After a day or two, we never wore the top half of our uniform to breakfast for fear of getting it dirty.

With a lot of the drill sergeants coming from a military background, tidiness was also expected, and if you didn't make your bed properly each morning, with the blanket carefully folded back underneath at the bottom, you were in trouble. If any of the cleaning women came into your room to find something out of place, you were hauled out of your classroom, brought over to clean it and barred from leaving the premises for two nights.

First class after breakfast was almost always drill and would be spent marching up and down the square for two hours or more to get ready for our passing-out parade at the end of our training period. We would then have a tea break and, having been split into five groups, the rest of the day would be spent in the classroom, studying the Irish language and various police duties and regulations in hour-long classes before and after lunch. These lessons were sometimes broken up by physical education in the gym or swimming lessons in the pool. At the end of each month we were told we would have exams and anyone who failed would have to repeat the month until he passed.

As soon as I got my first roster, I scanned it to see when swimming was on and had my togs and towel wrapped up under my desk in anticipation of my first time in the pool. As soon as class was over, I burst out of the door, whipped off my uniform in the changing rooms and ran up the stairs to the viewing balcony, about twelve feet over the pool. Without hesitation, I stood up on the handrail and dived straight into the pool below. I hadn't even touched the water before the sergeant, Reggie Barrett, roared at me and, upon my resurfacing, promptly threw me out of the class. I wasn't allowed back in the pool until the following week.

When I eventually lined up for swimming with all of the other recruits I was amazed to see that some of the lads were terrified of the water. I couldn't understand it. Although I'd been swimming from an early age, having taught myself, I soon realized that I didn't have the right stroke and had to be shown how to swim properly in Templemore. Despite getting off on a bad footing, as things progressed Sergeant Barrett and I got on really well and I enrolled in his lifesaving classes on Tuesday evenings. The class consisted of various exercises – duck diving, treading water, diving to the bottom of the pool and swimming along the floor – to improve our competence in the water before progressing to harder tasks. We were taught to both stand to attention and remove our uniform underwater. We'd swim up and down the pool fully dressed. We'd do it holding someone up out of the water. Finally, we would jump into the pool in full uniform and swim lengths while towing a fully clothed colleague with us.

As well as swimming, we did boxing as part of our physical training, and coach Evans Byrnes gave extracurricular boxing classes. I wasn't a particularly good boxer but had done a bit in Waterford and it was something else to do in the evenings.

Once classes were over at five, there was a scramble to get to the canteen for tea, which was invariably a big fry-up, and then another rush to get back to the rooms and strip out of our uniforms. If I didn't have a lifesaving or boxing class, I'd join the others in the daily race to get out the gates and down the town to the shop or, more often than not, to the pub. While I'd been worried about the smell of drink off my breath on that first day's drive to Templemore, I was soon spending my nights sprinting back up the main street with a gang of classmates in an effort to beat the 11 p.m. curfew. If you weren't in before eleven, there were serious consequences. Every so often an inspector would be present when we returned and on such occasions there would be a line of recruits naïvely holding their breath and trying to act sober as they signed back in.

Although I continued the habit of saving part of my wages, the rest of my money was spent in one of two places: the Templemore Arms Hotel or the Eagle Bar, both of which were a short sprint from the main gate. As we were paid (in cash) at the end of the month rather than weekly, money was short most of the time. When my mother sent me ten pounds for my nineteenth birthday I was the most popular man in the dormitory.

On Sunday mornings we had to go out to the yard and parade in two lines before our obligatory trip to Mass and, if you had a means of transport, you could go home for the day afterwards. After drinking heavily the night before, I spent one particular Sunday morning vomiting up green bile in the toilet at the back of Templemore church. Afterwards we were told that a room had been burgled during Mass and, as I had been seen leaving the church, I was the prime suspect. I was brought in by my superiors and interviewed about the robbery but they believed me when I told them the truth, and it turned out that the guy who reported me as being the main suspect was actually the culprit himself.

We were allowed home for three weekends during training, leaving on a Saturday morning to be back in on Sunday evening. I used to think I was great, going out in Waterford on those weekends. In my head, everybody knew I was a guard and had a new-found respect for me. In fairness, though I might have had delusions about how powerful I was, I wasn't as bad as one of the other recruits, who wore his uniform at home, raided a pub on one of his days off and nearly got sacked over it.

The fact that I was now a guard also brought me some unwanted attention in the local pubs, and one night I was cornered and called a pig by one of the local gougers. I knew that in my new position I couldn't retaliate, but the incident was quelled by an older man who intervened and bought me a drink. The next morning my brother Philly and I went back into town, found the gouger and warned him never to do it again.

Another time, I was at the bar in a local hotel when a former teacher of mine from the Christian Brothers walked in.

'Ah, Mr Lavery, I hear you're in the guards now —'

That was as far as he got. The same guy had nearly knocked me out in class a few years earlier so I stopped him and told him never to speak to me again, unless he wanted the same medicine he had been dishing out to his pupils for years.

The weekend trips home were also great for stashing up on home-made bread or other treats. One fellow brought back a bottle of poitín one time and we hid it behind a tree on the grounds. We'd sneak out along the back fence, stuff it under our jumpers and take a few swigs out of it before going down the town in the evenings. As we got more confident and used to the way the college worked, we began to push our luck when it came to staying out drinking. After Offaly won the All-Ireland Football Final replay in October I decided to sneak out with the Offaly lads to enjoy the homecoming celebrations and, after a quick tea, we got into a car and headed for Tullamore, forty miles away. We didn't arrive back in until around half past four the next morning so, to avoid detection, we parked the car down the road and climbed in over the back wall.

Although we sneaked into the college, up the stone steps, down along the corridors and into bed without being seen, we thought we had been rumbled the next morning on parade. The sergeant, Reggie Barrett, lined us up as usual before bellowing, 'I know there were men who left this place last night and came back late . . .'

We feared the worst until he looked at me and said, 'I know it wasn't you, Lavery . . .'

Although the Offaly lads were obviously under suspicion, we now knew he had no proof and we were off the hook.

Passing-out ceremonies in Templemore were always followed by a dinner dance. Parents and families would come for the morning ceremony and bring the newly passed-out garda into town or to nearby Thurles for lunch afterwards. Parents generally went home after lunch, while girlfriends stayed and went to the dinner dance that evening with the newly qualified garda on his last day before he was shipped off to a station somewhere around the country.

Sean Sweeney was in the class ahead of me. As he was from Malin Head in north Donegal, his parents didn't make the long trip down to his passing out so we went on a bender to Tramore Races that afternoon instead. When we came back drunk that evening, nothing would do me but to go into Sean's passing-out dance and, once inside, I noticed that one of the lads in my class was doing barman, so I became the beneficiary of plenty more free drink.

Sergeant Tierney was there with his wife and for some reason I decided to take her out dancing. I was so drunk, though, that she couldn't hold me up. Both of us ended up in a heap on the floor and two or three recruits were ordered to bring me to bed.

A few days later, out in the yard, one of the drill instructors started giving out about recruits making a show of themselves drinking. Just as I thought I was going to be thrown out of the guards altogether, he continued, 'They go down the town and they make a show of us in front of the public. At least there's men that come in here and they're not ashamed to do it in front of us. We had a man in here the other night who got drunk in front of everybody but he went to bed as soon as he was told . . .'

Somehow I was off the hook again, even if I didn't remember the night in question at all.

It rained on the day that my class was supposed to pass out, so we had no parade. Having spent months marching around the yard to be ready for it, we were disgusted. Now a fully fledged garda, I posed in my uniform with my mother and father either side of me for a formal photograph in the gym. That photo took pride of place in my mother's house ever after. My parents drove home after the dinner while the rest of us headed into Templemore town for more drink.

Early the next morning, with sore heads and hangovers, O'Malley's Midgets were bussed from Templemore into Dublin to the capital's main bus depot, Busáras. I can still remember an old Dub shouting, 'Look at the bleedin' rozzers!' as we legged it into the pub across the road from Busáras for a quick pint before saying our goodbyes and boarding various buses to begin our new careers.

# 3

# A border station

When they had announced in class two days earlier that Thomas Lavery would be going to Ballyconnell, I nudged the recruit sitting beside me and asked him where Ballyconnell was but he didn't know either. Another classmate told me that it was in County Cavan, 'near the border'. With the Troubles raging in the North, it turned out that a lot of us were being sent to the border: five to Ballyconnell, five to Swanlinbar and six to Clones.

On the bus north, I found myself sitting beside a young soldier, staring out the window at the names of the towns that we passed through . . . Navan, Kells, Virginia. Virginia – that stirred my memory. I had watched the TV series *The Virginian*. In all innocence, I asked the soldier next to me if it was where the cowboys lived. He nearly pissed himself laughing. Later, when we passed the Half Acre in Cavan town, he said, 'There's a few cowboys in there.'

On my arrival in Ballyconnell that evening, I headed for the bed and breakfast in Church Street, where I had been booked in to stay. Unlike modern B&Bs, there was no requirement back then from the tourism authority to maintain a certain standard in order to be allowed to run such an establishment and the house was an ordinary family home. I was shown into a bedroom about nine feet wide by nine feet long, containing three small beds and a wardrobe. It was only then that I realized I would be sleeping in the same room as two other guards and we would all be sharing the only wardrobe in the tiny room.

I threw my case onto my bed and, by way of introduction, the two older guards in the house took me up the town that night for a few bottles of stout. Conscious of my new role as a pillar of the community, and with my first day as a 'real' garda just around the corner, I was keeping an eye on the clock as we drank and chatted. As closing time approached, I stood up to leave. I didn't want to get caught for drinking after hours before I'd even started on the job.

'What are you talking about?' said my new colleagues, laughing. 'There's no closing time here!'

The next morning I realized I had forgotten to pack a toothbrush in my case and, with the stale smell of alcohol still on my breath, I walked out of the B&B and stood in the middle of the road, wondering where I could find one. A young country girl came cycling across the bridge and I stopped her and asked if she knew where I could buy a toothbrush. She told me she was just on her way to the chemist shop and I was welcome to join her. I took her up on the offer, bought the toothbrush and later made a date with the girl. I was beginning to like Ballyconnell already.

My unplanned toothbrush stop meant that I was a few minutes late for my first day at work and, despite being in the town only a few hours, I had already earned a bollocking from my sergeant. Later that day the new recruits were brought out to the edge of town in a patrol car to be shown the border between the Republic and Northern Ireland. I asked one of the local guards where the line was.

'What line?'

'The white line on the road to show where the border is.'

I wasn't joking. I was an innocent nineteen-year-old who had never been anywhere and I actually thought there would be a white line on the road that we weren't allowed to cross. The garda thought I was being a smartarse and I was in trouble again.

Back in 1972, Ballyconnell was tiny, with a population of around 200. Nestled at the foot of the Slieve Russell mountain, with the Woodford River hugging its back streets, Ballyconnell's main claim to fame was that it had won an award for being Ireland's tidiest town the year before. (It would do so again two years later.) However, lurking underneath the picture-postcard facade was an undercurrent of extreme violence and even murder. Ballyconnell lay just one mile from the border and, like most other border towns since the eruption of the Troubles, it had become a gateway for subversives into and out of Northern Ireland. IRA gangs would sneak weapons into the North which were used to attack military targets or kill British soldiers. On the other hand, the loyalist UVF and other Protestant paramilitaries would come in the opposite direction with the aim of killing Catholics. With gun smuggling, bombings and shootings an almost daily occurrence, Ballyconnell was a dangerous place to be a garda in the early seventies.

But none of that really concerned me. It wasn't that I was brave. It was simply that I hadn't a clue what was going on; had I understood, I probably would have been very afraid.

Life in Ballyconnell was quiet enough at the start. Us new recruits were mainly there to stop gun smuggling and to search vacant houses in the area. You might have to do vacant house searches one morning a week, to make sure the IRA weren't using them as safe houses, but a lot of the time was spent standing at a checkpoint along the border.

If there was a big incident, we would be issued a 'Cordon 22' notice from Monaghan and certain junctions would have to be manned on a twenty-four-hour basis until it was lifted. I'm sure many an illegal weapon went past our checkpoints in a coffin or a milk churn, or even tied to the underside of an animal in a herd of cattle, but we were innocent young fellas who hadn't a clue. We were just uniforms, really.

On the checkpoint one night, I was bored and decided that jumping over the checkpoint signs would be a good way of staying awake and keeping fit at the same time. This new fitness regime soon became a regular thing. But at half two one morning, I was running and jumping over these signs when I hit one of them and fell. Wearing heavy boots with metal tips in the heels was bad enough, but the clatter of them knocking the sign soon alerted the neighbours. A window of the pub down the road opened, and the lady of the house roared at me to 'cop myself on'. She told the sergeant about me the next day, and within a few weeks of my arriving in Ballyconnell the whole town knew me as the 'mad young guard from Waterford'.

My reputation was enhanced a while later while working on a checkpoint at the Diamond at the end of the main street as a local republican drank in the nearby Woodford Arms pub. Upon seeing me outside, he decided to come out in between drinks to hurl abuse at me before returning to the counter in a drunken stupor.

Eventually I got fed up with this and went into the pub and reminded the owner that it was an offence to serve a drunk on the premises and not to give him any more alcohol. Upon hearing this, the IRA man followed me out and abused me even more, so I grabbed him by the scruff of the neck and frogmarched him up Main Street as everyone on the street stopped and watched.

I can imagine what I must have looked like, all of five-feet-eight-and-a-half and built like a twig, marching the top Provo in the area through Ballyconnell by the throat. He was drunk and roaring and shouting as I brought him into the station, but almost as soon as I'd gone back to my checkpoint the senior garda on duty let him out.

Another night, I was walking past an alleyway when I heard a commotion. There had been a row in the local pub and there were a gang of men going to kill an IRA man down the lane. Unarmed and sober, I went down into the middle of them and told them all to fuck off home. I was lucky I wasn't killed.

That Christmas, my mother gave me some money she'd saved to help me buy a car so that I could go home more often to visit her. I collected my first car, a spanking-new little blue Mini, from Tony McCann, a car dealer in Carrick-on-Shannon, on 1 January 1973. It cost £840.

Now that I had my own car, I thought I had arrived.

While drink-driving carries obvious dangers and a huge antisocial stigma now, back then it wasn't given a second thought and it was commonplace to go to a dance, drink brandies and pints all night long, and then drive home. I remember stopping somebody for drink-driving once in my early days in Ballyconnell. At first, I tried to drive him home but he told me I was nothing but a 'bog man from Cork' so I brought him to the station. I explained the situation to the sergeant, but the driver was a famous Cavan inter-county footballer so nothing ever came of it.

One night in January 1973, half an hour after a colleague, Seamus Drury, and I had finished manning a checkpoint on the southern side of Aghalane Bridge outside Belturbet, the bridge was blown up for the second time in three months.

After it had initially been blown up by loyalist para-militaries a few months earlier, Cavan County Council rebuilt the bridge in December, but when a loyalist bomb killed two teenagers in Belturbet while I was at home for Christmas, and a series of IRA attacks were carried out in the North shortly afterwards, the loyalists blew it up again to cut off the IRA's favoured route across the border.

After helping to take an old woman out of her house because the explosion had blown the slates off her roof,

I was brought out to what remained of the bridge and told to 'guard the yellow road'. I was left standing there on my own, four miles from the nearest garda station, in the pitch dark, staring at a length of tape tied across the road with a cardboard sign saying 'Bomb' stuck to the middle of it. I was given orders to stop any cars coming from Belturbet heading north and divert them back through Ballyconnell and the concession road, which added twelve miles onto the journey, but I spent most of the night in the bushes.

Cars were few and far between but I was in terror, afraid of the UDA, the UVF or somebody coming out of the bushes and shooting me. I'm not particularly religious but I said about ten rosaries that night. I was terrified, a gobshite from down South who hadn't a clue what was going on, and it was only later that I realized that whoever had bombed the bridge had been waiting, watching for us to leave the checkpoint before blowing it up.

Another night, myself and Paddy McMorrow, on our way to the border in the patrol car, came across a British army jeep and a soldier standing out in the middle of the road looking at a map underneath a street light. Sent to set up a checkpoint in the North, he was obviously unaware his patrol had crossed the border. He was in very real danger of being shot by local IRA members if they saw him.

I walked around to the back of the jeep and pulled back its curtain to reveal five or six young soldiers armed to the teeth, sitting huddled together, terrified. Like me, they were probably only new recruits, maybe eighteen or nineteen years old, and they had no idea what they were doing.

Although I was young and unarmed, I had no qualms about telling the British officer to get himself and his men back into his own territory before they were killed, although I probably wasn't quite that polite.

At the time, the Irish government was taking border incursions very seriously and, despite our best efforts to conceal the incident, and therefore avoid the pile of paperwork that would follow, the news of a border incursion at Ballyconnell swept the area in a flash. The incident made it as far as the national news on RTÉ the next day and there were questions asked about it in the Dáil.

People were saying that I should have arrested the whole British patrol and brought them to the station but I knew that if I'd done that, we would have had a very serious situation on our hands. British soldiers were deemed legitimate targets by the IRA and shootings were commonplace. If the local Provos had heard there was a group of British soldiers, especially an officer, in the station, they would have surrounded the place and wiped us all out.

Brought before the sergeant in charge, an inspector and a superintendent the following morning, I was asked why I hadn't made an arrest. I replied that I thought it was better to tell them to go back into the North as we'd never have been able to secure them at the station. Tom Hughes, the local inspector and a gentleman, winked at me and that was the end of it.

When the older gardaí had laughed at me for worrying about closing time on my first night in the pub in Ballyconnell, I got my first insight into the drinking culture in the job along the border. With little else to do, no family or friends around to spend time with, nights in the pub with colleagues and locals would soon be a regular occurrence.

Single young guards usually spent their money on drink and cars, so seeing a car belonging to one in a ditch after a night out was nothing unusual in those days. Looking back, I don't know how we got away with it.

After a few months in Ballyconnell I moved out of the B&B and stayed with a Protestant woman named Mrs Wright in Milltown, eight miles away. Mrs Wright was a widow and her children were much older than me and had moved out. She was an absolute lady and when I moved in she treated me like her son. As well as feeding me and looking after me, Mrs Wright would have my uniform spotless. Back in those days, we wore shirts with studs in the collars and she used so much starch on my shirt collars that they'd be stiff as a rod by the time she was finished with them. While some of the guards at the time took no pride in their appearance, sauntering around with long hair, white socks and dandruff on their uniforms, I was always dressed immaculately, with my uniform clean and tidy and my shoes polished until you could see the shine off them a mile away. Thanks to Mrs Wright, I was one of the best-turned-out guards in Ireland. I might have been drunk some of the time, but I was gleaming.

Towards the end of the summer I went to a dinner dance in Ballinamore and picked up my blind date in my brand-new car. I wore a wine Crombie coat, a crisp white shirt and a wine tie. With my new car and flashy clothes, at twenty I was every inch the Dapper Dan. I had three brandies to 'settle the nerves' while waiting for my date. I drank all night at the event. Then, after leaving the girl home, I wrapped my new car around the pillar of a gate.

I was asleep in the car for a few hours before a farmer who lived nearby pulled me out of it, brought me in and gave me tea.

I explained that I'd only just bought the car and didn't want the station to find out what had happened, so the farmer hauled the car in off the road, took the number plates off and, at around eight o'clock that morning, I banged on the front door of the man I'd bought it from.

Tony McCann had been to the same dinner dance the night before and was in as bad a state as I was, but we brought the car over to his brother's place to see what he could do. As he cut off the roof and welded on a new one, we went to the pub, where I drank myself stupid watching the Irish rugby team play Scotland on TV. I ended the night by being marched up and down the stairs of Tony's house by a friend of his wife's (who happened to be my blind date's sister), in an effort to make me vomit and sober up.

In my drunken haze, I thought that I had gotten away without anyone knowing about the crash but I had been spotted when I'd been asleep behind the wheel and one of the locals spread the word that the 'mad young guard from Waterford' had written off his car and I was in trouble again.

Having wrecked the car my mother had helped me buy, I had to work overtime for the next six months to pay for the loan and the repair bill. Rather than tell my mother the truth, I delayed going home by saying that I was so busy on the border that I simply couldn't get time off.

There were five or six new recruits in every border station and we were easy to pick out with our different accents and tight haircuts. Any time you went to a dance you'd see twenty-five or thirty shaved heads. At the time, there were no discos or nightclubs in Ireland. The 'ballrooms of romance' or the local dance halls were your options – women to the left, men to the right.

While the young guards were a big hit with the local girls, the local republicans weren't particularly fond of us. One night at a dance in the Hillgrove Hotel in Monaghan, I was chatting to a guard from Cobh at the bar when a republican stole his drink. Not wanting to make a big thing out of it, I told the Cobh fella not to worry about it and bought him another one.

A few minutes later I was standing at a urinal in the gents when I got a dig in the back of the head. I managed to give one of my attackers a good slap before being knocked to the ground but looked up to see a couple of the local republicans' boots flying at me. They gave me a good beating, kicking me around the place, and as I was trying to protect myself with my arm, one of them broke my wrist with a boot.

I was brought to Monaghan Hospital and was lying in bed when my old Templemore classmate Gussy Keating, who was stationed in nearby Clones, came to visit me and told me the chief superintendent, J. P. McMahon, was coming to see me. Knowing that it was unlikely that my story would be believed as I was drunk, and that I'd most probably get a reprimand, I jumped out the hospital window, got into the car and went off to Clones with Gussy.

I woke up the next morning with my hand hanging limp and had to drive one-armed to Cavan Hospital, where they patched me up with a plaster cast. I arrived back into the station that afternoon, ready to tell them a story of how I slipped in Mrs Wright's, but the sergeant had already heard the real story from two gardaí who had been at the dance and I was sent home to Waterford to recover.

Despite the dangers of working along the border, most of which I was blissfully unaware of, I grew to love Ballyconnell and its people, and in my twenty-two months posted there I found that the locals had a lot of time for me too. As I was the youngest garda in the town, a lot of the kids in the area would talk to me and have a laugh.

There was one small kid in particular I got on really well with. Niall Crowe was only about four years old and not in school yet, so almost every day that I'd walk up the town, he'd jump out from a side street and pull the tail of my uniform coat, looking for a chase. I'd often give him a few bob to get himself sweets in the shop or let him wear my garda hat for a few minutes as he pretended to arrest me on my way to work.

After doing a night shift, I woke up one afternoon and strolled into town to be hit with the news that the little fella was dead. He had gone missing earlier that morning and most of the town had spent the day searching for him. He was found floating face down in the river that flowed at the back of his house.

When I got over the initial shock, I was overcome with immense frustration. I'd been off duty and in bed after doing nights but I felt that if I'd been in the town that day it wouldn't have happened. Maybe he would have followed me up the street and not gone near the river. Maybe I could have saved him, pulled him from the water. I'd done the lifesaving course in Templemore and was probably the only one in the town who knew anything about first aid at the time. But I'd been asleep, useless, and it took me a long time to get over it.

Apart from activity arising out of the Troubles, there was little routine crime in Ballyconnell, and most of the guards in the area weren't interested in bringing people to court for offences like having no road tax or car insurance. There was always the exception, though, and I remember one particular older garda making me stop a local for having no tax disc once.

The driver received about ten summonses but by then I had gotten to know who was who locally and I knew the man simply hadn't got the money to pay the fines, so I spent a long time doing a mitigation for him, visiting his house and filling in forms to present in court. He got away with only having to pay three pounds. I was delighted but I never did it again in my life. The only time I was ever in court after that was as a witness.

In October 1973 I was walking into the garda station to start duty at ten o'clock one night while a colleague stopped cars outside. I knew one of the drivers stopped at the checkpoint and went over to say hello when I noticed a stunning-looking girl sitting behind him in the back seat and began making small talk with her. I asked her where she was going and she replied that she was on her way down the street to Danny Reilly's pub.

As quick as a flash, I went into the station and asked the guard who was finished at ten if he would work on until six the next morning if I did his six-to-two shift the next day. When he said he would, I put on my leather jacket, turned on my heels, jumped into my welded-together car and followed them down the town.

Susan Donohoe was seventeen and I was three years older when we met that night. After talking to her all night and me buying drink like it was going out of fashion, we started dating. Susan lived about five miles across the border in Dernagore, near Derrylin, with her parents, five sisters and four brothers on farmland that stretched down to the Woodford River, which divided North and South. They lived in a cul-de-sac and soon got used to British soldiers coming into their yard in the dead of night. Although as guards we were warned not to cross the border for our own safety, I made many trips along the concession road after that to collect Susan and bring her to the pub or to local dances.

In any case, despite the informal ban on going into the North, like most of the young guards I was forever going across the border, shopping and buying petrol and tyres in Northern Ireland because it was cheaper. Every Thursday a few of us would take a trip to Enniskillen to the market where we'd buy eight-track stereo tapes and have a few drinks in a Protestant pub across the road until the UDR stopped us one day and, in an effort to show us who was boss that side of the border, took everything out of the boot and left it on the road.

Apart from drinking and playing the odd game of poker, the only other real pastime I had in Ballyconnell was going to watch the odd game of Gaelic football. I'd drive to Cavan or Monaghan to watch inter-county games and was driving through Belturbet on the way to a Cavan match when a local garda, Charlie Cunnea, stopped me. With no garda car assigned to Belturbet and the nearest patrol car eight miles away, Charlie was in the process of scouring the area for a lift when he spotted a face he knew and asked me to drive him the four miles to Aghalane Bridge.

Although most of the bridge was now gone, there was still a narrow pathway across the river that locals used to walk into town and get their daily shopping or have a few pints. One of these locals, Johnny Maguire, had gone for a few drinks the night before, and when walking back across the bridge he'd stumbled and fallen into the river below. Somebody had reported seeing a body in the water and Charlie had been told to see if he could find him.

When we arrived at the bridge, a body could be seen clearly, floating downriver. We didn't really know what to do. Even though I was off duty, I ended up stripping to my underpants, getting into the water and swimming out. I don't know why, but seeing the body in the water didn't scare me. I simply swam across, pulled the man up out of the water and, using the skills learned in Templemore, turned to swim back towards Charlie on the bank with the body under my arm.

By now a handful of other guards had arrived – including the local sergeant – and there was pandemonium on the river bank. I was just about to haul the man's body out of the water when the sergeant bellowed at me.

'The other side!'

By leaving the body on the opposite bank, it became Northern Ireland's problem and this saved the sergeant a lot of paperwork and administrative headaches. The British army and the RUC helicopters had to be brought in and there was huge commotion in the area afterwards.

Johnny Maguire's was the first body I ever pulled out of the water. I was twenty years old that day but I still remember his name. I had no idea back then that he would be the first of many.

On New Year's Day 1974, having driven my patched-up car for long enough, I traded it in for a new Fiat 124, but the Fiat didn't last much longer than the Mini had. A first off-road incident, where I drunkenly drove into a field, saw the vehicle sustain superficial scrapes and damage that was fixable. But a drunken drive home from a wedding, four months after buying it, ended with a U-shaped hole left in the engine when I hit a telegraph pole head-on near Brackley Lake. When they tried to get me out of the car this time they couldn't wake me.

At the time, sergeants from all over the country used to be sent up to the border for two months and would be put into a unit to observe how it operated. They'd get a special allowance for this 'temporary transfer' but none of them had any interest in being there and would often fall asleep in the patrol car as you drove on night duty.

My favourite pastime during those periods was to slam on the brakes and wake the temporary sergeant up by banging his head off the dashboard, or at least by giving him a little bit of whiplash.

'What the fuck?' one of them said as I slammed on.

'Did you not see that fuckin eejit on the wrong side of the road with no lights?' I said.

At around five o'clock one morning I drove a Limerick sergeant over to Butlersbridge, which was outside our patrol area, and pulled in at a lake where, much to the delight of the sergeant, I opened the boot and pulled out a couple of fishing rods that Mrs Wright had given me to help ease the boredom of the country beat. But the first cast I threw out saw the front half of the rod break off, go flying into the lake and get stuck. The sergeant from Limerick looked at me in bewilderment as I began to take off my uniform at the side of the road, stripping down to my underpants before swimming out into the lake to retrieve the rod.

The lads told me afterwards that the sergeant was worried that if anything had happened to me, he would have had a very hard time explaining what he was doing watching me swimming in my underwear in a lake outside our area instead of patrolling the local roads.

But there was a dangerous side to working on the border too. In my time there, loyalists murdered a local butcher, Louis Leonard, in Derrylin, leaving him hanging up in the freezer with a hook, normally used to hang meat, stuck into his head. There was also a lethal IRA gang operating in the area and pretty soon things began to get very serious. Guards on checkpoints were stripped and beaten and a sergeant from Cork was left with permanent ear damage after being hit with a gun.

Straight after killing Colonel George Saunderson, a British war hero turned headmaster – shooting him in a school kitchen during an infamous raid in April 1974 – the gang drove past the checkpoint where I was on duty. I stood out in the road at the checkpoint but the gang didn't stop, just crashed straight through and kept going. Afterwards I discovered that a few minutes before coming up to my checkpoint they had held a gun to another man's head when he tried to block their escape with his truck. Looking back, I can see I was in danger every day but I never really thought about it at the time.

People couldn't understand how this IRA gang could strike, kill whoever they wanted, and then disappear off the road and not be seen again until their next raid. But there was a lot of sympathy for the IRA in the border counties and there were plenty of people willing to help them and willing to provide food and a good hiding place for them.

In one of their regular vacant-house searches, the guards in nearby Ballinamore came across the gang. One of the Provos fired a shot at an unarmed local officer, Sergeant Monaghan. The bullet went through his lapel and hit him in the ear. Shooting at a garda upped the stakes considerably and we were on the road for three days without sleep trying to find them. The gang stole a car from a farmer to escape in, but to give them a better chance of getting away the car wasn't reported stolen by its owner for a day. There was a big cross-country chase but they got away from the guards in Mayo, got through another checkpoint in Leitrim and were on the run for a long time before being captured.

# 4

## In at the deep end

With the Troubles getting worse as time went on, and
gardaí now beginning to get caught in the crossfire, I began
to look for a way to get off the border and started to train
hard for the garda boxing championships. Most of the
best garda boxers were based around Dublin at the time
and were given dispensation to train and prepare for fights.
Having boxed in Templemore and as a youngster in Waterford, I figured that if I fought well at the championships
there might be a chance that I could be transferred to
Dublin and get away from the border.

When I applied to go to the championships, however,
the local sergeant made little of my notions and told me
that he couldn't let me go to box in Dublin because I'd get
knocked out. To make his point, with a hefty weight advantage and towering over me at well over six feet tall, he
challenged me to take him on for a round in front of the
other lads. I knew that if I lost he would make a laughing
stock out of me and that if I beat him things would be
even worse, so I bit my lip and declined his offer, much to
his delight.

Shortly afterwards, though, one of the lads in the station handed me the weekly internal circular and pointed to

a page advertising for applicants for a new Garda Sub-Aqua Unit. This unit was being created after vital evidence had been lost from the MV *Claudia*, a boat that had carried five tons of weapons donated to the IRA by Libya's Colonel Gaddafi into Ireland in March 1973.

The boat was boarded by members of the Irish Naval Service in Helvick Head, Waterford, but the evidence disappeared when IRA leader Joe Cahill threw a large package overboard. Part of this package was a black box containing false passports, a list of contact names and addresses throughout Europe, and £40–50,000 in cash, a huge amount considering the average wage at the time was around £1,000 per year. An army diver was sent down to search for the package a few days later but by then local fishermen had marked the spot with a buoy and made sure the package got to its intended destination.

The incident led to a question in the Dáil as to why the gardaí had no divers and it was explained that, while there had been a handful of sports divers in the Garda Sub-Aqua Club since 1966, they had given up diving on the job in 1971 when they didn't get enough subsistence to cover their costs and were forced to use and replace their own equipment on any dives they were required to do. After much deliberation the government decided to set up an official Garda Sub-Aqua Unit in 1974.

'You're a good swimmer, why don't you go for that?' asked my colleague as I read through the circular.

A few weeks after sending in my application for the unit, I was brought to Dublin for a medical and then to the ALSAA swimming pool across from Dublin airport with the other applicants for a first batch of tests in the water. I had no problem with these tests, which mainly consisted of swimming up and down the pool, both on the surface and underwater.

From forty-seven applicants, I was one of a dozen chosen for further training and was given a temporary transfer to Dublin for the next three months. I had cousins who lived at Moyglare Stud Farm in Kildare so I moved into their house while Susan, who was by then my steady girlfriend, moved to Dublin in search of work and stayed in a flat with her sisters.

Of the dozen chosen for training, I was the youngest, with most of the others married and all of them already stationed in the city. Indeed, Louis Baldwin and myself, both from Waterford, were the only rural-based guards to be selected. Brian Cusack, Sean Sheridan and John Hales of the Irish Underwater Council were brought in to train us as sports divers and we were given some lectures on the physics of diving before doing anything in the water.

We first learned to snorkel and use fins in the pool at Dublin airport: with the instructors throwing them into the deep end, we'd have to take a breath, dive in and put them on at the bottom of the pool before resurfacing. Once we were competent with the fins and snorkels, we were given diving cylinders to put on so we could get used to the weight. Then we were shown how to use them.

Before we were able to swim outside in the sea we were each given a wetsuit. Made from thin neoprene material, a wetsuit allows the water in, with the water inside the suit supposedly heated up by the temperature of your body. Nowadays, kids use wetsuits to paddle or swim in pools and you can buy them in Penneys or any other large retailers, but in 1974 our suits came in a kit form. With the neoprene cut into a pattern by one of the tailors in the garda uniform stores, we each had to stitch, glue and tape the sleeves and legs onto our own suit in the airport gym.

A good wetsuit will give you maybe half an hour before its benefits start to fade. A drysuit, however, is what we should have had and is much better for open-water diving. Like a big waterproof Babygro, sealed at the cuffs and neck, a drysuit locks out all the water and you can wear thermal layers, or even your ordinary clothes, underneath it to keep you warm in freezing conditions.

Lead was scrounged from the roof of a demolished garda station in Crumlin and weight belts were made to help us sink down in the water on dives, although life jackets to help us come back up were deemed a luxury we didn't need.

Our first outdoor dives were in Bullock Harbour, in Dalkey, where we spent days learning how to jump in off the pier with a cylinder and mask on. We were taught to jump in with one hand on our mask and the other clamped over our mouths so that our regulators didn't shatter our teeth upon impact with the water. A regulator is the mouthpiece used to reduce pressurized air or breathing gases supplied from the cylinder on the diver's back. (Right from the start I understood that this regulator was vital to keeping me alive underwater and I made sure mine stayed in pristine condition, filling it with water in the sink every night to wash out the salt before storing it safely. Later on, I would see plenty of divers get into trouble after failing to maintain their equipment to the same standard.)

We used fins to snorkel from Bullock Harbour out to the famous Forty Foot swimming spot in Sandycove, and we also did breath-held dives down along some lobster-pot lines around the rocks there. After three months of training in Dublin, we were brought over to Clare Island, near Clew Bay in Mayo, where we did some deep supervised dives of around 130 feet in clear water.

These deeper dives brought a new danger – decompression sickness, or 'the bends'. On land, the air around us has a pressure of 14.7 psi (pounds per square inch), or one atmosphere, but when you're breathing compressed air from a scuba tank, for every thirty-three feet you dive you add another 14.7 psi to the air in your lungs and high-pressure gases begin to dissolve into liquid in your body. When this pressure is released on the way back to the surface, however, these gases form bubbles. If these bubbles don't disperse before you hit the surface they can travel to various parts of your body and cause anything from joint pain to paralysis and even death, and each dive can affect you in a different way.

In layman's terms, trying to avoid the bends is like shaking a fizzy drink and then trying to open the bubbling liquid without letting any of it overflow. As the bubbles form in your body on the way up, you have to take your time and come to the surface slowly enough to expel those bubbles, or 'lift the cap off the Coke bottle'. In order to do this, we had to make decompression stops on the way back to the surface on these deep dives.

Although I'd stopped drinking during the week in an effort to make the diving team, I would still have a few pints with my cousins at the weekend. One of the instructors, Brian Cusack, was pretty regimental and a stickler for rules and my wilder side didn't exactly correspond with his notion of how a garda should conduct himself. After one of our regular Friday evening debriefing sessions in a tent on Clare Island, Brian pulled me aside and gave me a talking to.

'You won't make it in this unit, Lavery. You're mad.'

After logging the requisite hours and passing our tests, we were qualified sports divers and I was a fully fledged member of the first official Garda Sub-Aqua Unit.

The original 'dirty dozen' also included former Garda Sub-Aqua Club member Neil Bracken, who was our first sergeant, John Harrington from west Cork, Louis Baldwin from Waterford, Dubliners Padraig Tunney and Mick Carr, Larry Keane from Offaly, Donal Gibbons from Donegal, Jim Flood from Longford, Matt Lennon from Louth, Kerryman Mossy Moriarty and Pascal Scott from Cork. (Pascal later went into acting and is best known for playing Sergeant Dick O'Toole in the TV sitcom *Killinaskully*.)

We may have been certified divers, but we were still utter novices and if we knew little about diving, we knew even less about diving for bodies. Nonetheless, shortly after passing our tests, we were sent to Galway to search for three men who had fallen out of a boat somewhere between Clifden and Omey Island. The trio were on their way back from watching Galway play Dublin in the All-Ireland Final in a pub on the mainland when they got into difficulty and their currach capsized in the middle of the night.

Our transportation was two vans and drivers from the garda transport division. One was for the diving gear and the other for us divers – and a stack of beer cans to celebrate our passing out as members of the garda 'elite'. There was a bit of pride attached to being in the new diving unit, and upon stopping in Ballinasloe for something to eat, I could hear one of the drivers telling the barman that he was going down to the search and pretending he was one of the divers.

When we got to Clifden the horse fair was on and there was a big commotion about our presence. The legendary actor Peter O'Toole offered us the use of his house, possibly to make up for the fact that he was in trouble with the local guards for being drunk and disorderly at the fair. He stayed with friends when we moved in. O'Toole's was a fine big house on the Sky Road with views out over the Atlantic Ocean. Apparently, when the local county council planners ruled that the house would have to be built behind a hill instead of on top of it, O'Toole simply got rid of the hill altogether to get the views he wanted.

With the house to ourselves, at breakfast every morning we would each give the transport drivers, Ken and Mick, 50p and after dropping us off at the dive site they would head into town to buy meat and vegetables to rustle up a big stew for dinner later that evening. Ken and Mick would meet the local butcher for a few drinks and, after telling him they were doing the 'deep diving in the evening time', would get a good deal on the meat every day.

There were two stuntmen living on the tiny Omey Island at the time. Pascal Whelan had spent seven years touring Australia with his own stunt show and pocketed enough money to buy a house in New Zealand. But after a friend died during one of his shows, he gave it all up, returned to Omey in 1974, bought a charter boat and fished and dived in the area with his brother. Pascal insisted on helping us with the dives and, as he probably had as much experience underwater as we had, we let him join the search.

We tried to work out where the men had launched their little currach to go across to the island but there was no way of knowing how far it would have drifted off course in the dark or where it may have capsized.

On a dive with John Harrington and Louis Baldwin one day, I was swimming through a gap in some kelp when suddenly something huge flashed past me in the water. Certain it was a shark, I surfaced on the wrong side of the reef and started waving frantically to our boat in the distance. We were always worried about sharks out in the ocean and all I wanted to do was get into the boat before I was eaten.

I swam over and the lads pulled me aboard, thinking I had found something. But when I told them what happened they started laughing as they'd seen a school of dolphins swim past seconds earlier. As I began to catch my breath in the boat, the dolphins began to dive down and swim around the other two lads, who both had the same reaction as me and began to panic. We eventually got them into the boat and called off the dive for the day. I learned later that dolphins will sometimes play with you in the water and have been known to playfully hit divers in the stomach and drive the regulator out of their mouth.

After diving every day, we had a few pints at night in Clifden, where the Whelans would regale us with tales about working alongside motorcycle stuntman Evel Knievel and various Hollywood stars. An innocent twenty-one-year-old, I just passed off their stories as bravado but later on I learned that they were true. Indeed, Pascal Whelan gave up the fishing and went back to Australia to be a stunt double for Paul Hogan in the film *Crocodile Dundee* a few years later. Peter O'Toole also held the bar in the palm of his hand with movie stories at night although the local guards had plenty of their own about him too.

In the middle of our second week in Clifden, I found the seagull engine from the missing boat and a photo of me standing on the rocks with it appeared in the *Irish Press* the day after. My mother kept the clipping in a scrap book in the house for years after.

Even though everything was in our favour during that search – visibility was great and the weather was good – we were simply inexperienced and, having just finished our training as sports divers, we didn't know anything about how to search underwater. Although we stayed almost a fortnight we didn't find the bodies of the three missing men. Instead, all three were washed up on various parts of the shore almost a month later.

We left Clifden and headed to the seaside resort town of Kilkee in County Clare, where the European Spear Fishing Championships were being held in Irish waters for the first time. Every morning divers from as far afield as Bulgaria, Malta, Spain, Italy, Portugal, Yugoslavia and the UK would line their boats up along the beach and head to sea. Each diver had a little spear gun on his belt and after diving down and stalking the fish for a few seconds he would shoot it and send it back up on a line to a float on the surface. The diver with the most fish speared within a certain period would be crowned European champion.

Brought down to supervise and as cover if any of the divers got into difficulty, we were to keep an eye on things from our boats as competitors dived on a single breath. Although there is no danger of getting the bends on a single-breath dive, we were there in case one of the divers passed out from 'deep-water blackout', which can be caused by taking several very deep breaths in an effort to fill the lungs just before a dive, leading to a reduced supply of oxygen to the brain.

The winner of the competition that year was a little Italian called Massimo Scarpati. While the Irish divers Shane Gray and Ray Dunne could go down to sixty feet on one breath, Scarpati had little weights in his wetsuit and was getting to depths of around a hundred feet and caught sixty-five fish to win the competition outright. The Spaniard in second place caught the biggest fish that year, which weighed in at a whopping eighteen pounds. When he went up to collect his prize I noticed he was limping. José Amengual had arthritis in one leg and could barely walk, but he could hold his breath for over two and a half minutes underwater.

When the competition was over, we all went on the beer in Kilkee, where Sergeant Bracken mapped out an exciting career path for us, telling us that we were going to be an elite diving crew that would be responsible for the whole country and would be getting a big specially designed bus from Belgian coach builders Van Hool to accommodate us and our diving equipment. I was twenty-one, getting to travel around the country, diving in the mornings and having a few pints in various hotels and bars in the evening. Life was looking up.

# 5

# Tragedy in Donegal

We might have been an elite team of gardaí, but we still didn't know where we were going to be stationed. News finally filtered through that the new Garda Sub-Aqua Unit was to be based with the Defence Unit at Garda Headquarters in the Phoenix Park. This was the nerve centre of An Garda Síochána, a huge complex, home to everything from human resources to transport, and where you would find every level of officer from ordinary gardaí, like us, to the garda commissioner and his assistant commissioners.

There was also a small hospital on site where a doctor and a couple of nurses were based. If a guard from down the country was misbehaving or missing work, through alcohol or anything else, he was sent up to the hospital and given the once-over by the garda doctor. If he was bad enough he'd be temporarily posted to headquarters so that he could be kept an eye on or sent for rehab to St Patrick's Hospital.

I didn't know it at the time but being put on the Defence Unit, or 'the gate', was regarded by some as a punishment sentence for gardaí who had done something wrong, so immediately four of the older lads left the diving unit and went back to their stations. That left the team with just eight divers to cover the whole country.

My cousins in Moyglare agreed to have me stay with them on a more permanent basis. Even though she had a full house, my cousin Kathleen Flynn would have a dinner on the table for eight or nine of us every evening and my laundry was always spick and span, just like it was in Mrs Wright's in Ballyconnell.

As I had wrecked my second car, I got the bus in and out from Maynooth to Parkgate Street until I could afford another one. I was waiting for a bus one day when I spotted my former teacher 'Birdy', the Christian Brother who had once leathered me in front of the class, standing at a bus stop further along. I waited until he was just about to board his bus before running at him from behind and 'helping' him up the steps with a hefty shove. As he entered the bus head first, I turned and sprinted down O'Connell Street, delighted to have exacted my revenge.

If we weren't called out to dives or searches, life in the Phoenix Park was pretty monotonous. On the Defence Unit, a sergeant and seven men started each eight-hour shift. Two went to the old Garda Technical Bureau on St John's Road, near Heuston Station, one went to the garage, which always had an armed garda on duty because it housed the cars of various government ministers as well as the presidential car, while the rest of us went to the gate of the headquarters complex.

Working on the gate consisted of standing in front of a barrier and lifting it up and down to let other guards or visitors in and out. We also had to log who came and went.

One day a garda I knew arrived in at about ten to seven in the morning and said, 'Mark me in there at half six, Tom.' Just as I was about to scribble his name in the book, the sergeant on duty called me over and advised me never to sign anyone in or out on the wrong time. Within half an hour a patrol car arrived looking for the guard as he had been involved in a hit and run earlier.

The sentry box at the barrier was open to the elements but behind it there was a narrow corridor, leading to a small building which housed a locker room, a toilet and a little room with an open fire and a cooker. That was where we spent most of our time. The guard on gate duty would sit on a chair looking out the window of the building and if a car drove up to the gate he would go outside to lift up the barrier and let them through. Every morning in winter, a little man named Charlie from the Board of Works would come in to headquarters at six o'clock and set the fires for all the officers so that they would be blazing by the time they came to work. But there was no such privilege for the fellas on the gate.

In the room behind the barrier somebody would have to go over to the yard at the end of each shift, get a bucket of turf and stack the fire again for the next lads on duty. One guard seemed oblivious to this unwritten rule. He would hatch over the fire all day and if he was finished at midnight you could be sure that the last bit of turf would burn out at 11.59 and there wouldn't be a sod left for the next crew.

On the right-hand side as you passed our gate and entered Garda Headquarters there was a kind of canteen where a self-taught chef, Ned Moriarty, was based and we'd sometimes go in there for dinner while the guards living on site would eat there all the time. Above 'Moriarty's Mess' there were a few small rooms – like chalets or small dorms – where some of the older single guards lived, and more of them lived in another building nicknamed 'the bogside' round the back.

There were two members of the diving unit put on each shift of the Defence Unit. With the last two divers on their day off, and rotating shifts to cover the others, it meant that these two would be on overtime if we were called out to a diving job. The ordinary guards would be delighted whenever we got called out as it meant that they too would have to work overtime to cover us.

With little to do on the gate, we divided the time between us, which meant we all had to do just over an hour and a half each at the barrier. The rest of each shift was spent 'patrolling' the depot. After a while on the gate, I started getting clever. Instead of coming in at four, I'd come in at quarter to four and be first on the gate. I'd stay there, lifting the barrier and signing people in until quarter to six and then that was me finished with the gate for the evening. I'd pass the time by going to visit the drivers from transport division who brought us down the country and became good friends with Sergeant Vinny Hyland, who worked in the garage and also managed the garda soccer team.

Duty on the old Technical Bureau on St John's Road was a handy job because the gate was locked and nobody ever came in. If I was on nights there, I'd spend the time sitting reading old murder files and looking at black and white photographs. As there were no computers for keeping records in those days, they used to keep the hands of unidentified people down there, stored in jars of formaldehyde. It might have made it a bit eerie at night, although it never really bothered me.

May Murray's pub was close by, and if I was on the evening shift, myself and the other garda on duty would take turns to go for a few pints before going home. With the bar in such close proximity and not much said about drinking on the job, there was no shortage of heavy drinkers working in and around Garda Headquarters. When you did your stint on the gate, the canteen was just round the corner and, as it offered a full bar, which was open around the clock, it was common practice to have a few pints before you went home every day. Since most of the others in the diving unit were already married and had families and homes in Dublin, I found myself surrounded by guards much older than me, but because I'd been used to drinking with older lads in Waterford, I never really thought much about it.

Sometimes towards the end of my shift I'd nip into the bar, turn down my walkie-talkie and sit in the corner with a pint. Not much notice was ever paid to guards drinking in uniform in the canteen as nobody really knew who was on duty and who wasn't. You might have someone from the Garda Band in one corner and somebody else coming in off driver's detail in another. If you were working on the evening shift and had done your two hours on the gate before patrolling around the depot, you could easily slip up to the canteen, nip in the back door, drink until two in the morning and drive home.

Most evenings I'd have a few drinks, but sometimes I'd stay in the bar and play pool with guards coming in off other shifts, or guards who were supposed to be out patrolling the depot or doing something else, and it often led to me not going home until very late. There were often arguments between guards and the barman over not being served. One night a drunk guard ran down to our little room at the back of the sentry box asking for a brush to beat the barman with. What he didn't realize was that myself and the sergeant on duty, who had been transferred to the gate for giving his previous inspector a thump, had been having a sneaky pint in the canteen when the incident occurred and had just scrambled back to our post because the row broke out. Irate at having missed his few pints, the sergeant went ballistic and sent the culprit home.

One Christmas morning I was on the gate when one of the lodgers, a guard known as 'The Slat', came over for a chat. The Slat had something wrong with his toe but rather than waste money going to the doctor's, he simply cut a hole in the top of his shoe and bought a bottle of whiskey instead, which he proceeded to drink as he regaled me with a story of how he'd scored the winning point for Kerry in a previous All-Ireland. Young and innocent, I lapped it up and believed him until I heard him tell the same story to somebody else with a totally different ending.

In the space of two years I'd gone from running in the gate of Templemore dreading the thought of being caught with alcohol on my breath to not wanting to leave the bar at Garda HQ after work. In the early days, I never drank when I was on the midnight-to-eight shift. I rationalized it by telling myself that after being up all night, I wouldn't need a few pints to go to sleep. Later on there were mornings when I left the gate at eight o'clock and headed down to an early house on the quays in Dublin to continue drinking with another guard.

After a while, one of the guards who lived over Moriarty's Mess gave me a key to his room and whenever he was away driving a government minister down the country I would sleep in there between shifts. As there were no en suites in these rooms, if you needed to pee in the night you had to go down the stone steps and walk out across the yard to the toilet. To avoid this midnight trek, the guard in the room next door, nicknamed 'The Rod', had his own system in place. The Rod was a big drinker and every night that I stayed in the room I'd hear him walking up and down his room for about ten minutes before hearing the distinctive sound of urine being sprayed into a metal bucket. I'd then hear a sliding noise before he went to bed and snored his head off.

It was only later, while on the barrier one night, that I discovered what the sliding noise was. I happened to be standing outside the sentry box when I heard the noise and looked over to see The Rod slide up the sash window of his room before throwing out the contents of his bucket. Unfortunately for a particular sergeant whose parking space was underneath The Rod's window, his car was drenched with a bucket of steaming piss most nights.

The sergeant used to change his car every year and still couldn't figure out why each one went rusty.

As the only cars that ever came into Garda HQ at night were patrol cars looking to fill up with petrol in the garage, or guards on the beat in town looking for a few late drinks in the canteen, we would usually leave one non-drinker on duty to look after things when we slipped up to the canteen. One night when one of the guards on the gate had a bit of a retirement function in the canteen there was no 'pioneer' available, so we simply left the barrier up and went for a few pints. When we returned at five o'clock in the morning the barrier was still up and there were about a dozen cattle wandering around the depot, shitting everywhere. The cattle belonged to local farmers who had grazing rights in the park and we spent the next couple of hours drunkenly trying to herd them out and clearing up the cow shit before the arrival of the office staff.

Having been involved in a couple of small search dives for evidence, including one where we dived in the river Liffey to look for a calculator that had been taken in a house raid, the Sub-Aqua Unit's first real call-out came in January 1975 when a fishing trawler, the *Evelyn Marie*, went down off the Donegal coast. Having set sail from Burtonport village in Donegal, the trawler was on its way into Killybegs with a haul of fish when it struck a treacherous stretch of rocks off Rathlin O'Beirne Island, leaving all six crew members missing at sea.

The day after the tragedy, I heard news on the radio that

the bodies of two of the men had been found floating in the water with their life jackets on backwards. Shortly after, we were sent to Donegal to search for the others.

Despite having been promised our own customized bus with separate compartments for the diving gear, we travelled to that search in an old banger of a Bedford minibus which had been used to ferry guards up and down to Portlaoise Prison on security duties. A second Bedford van was loaded to the gills with our diving gear and it pulled a trailer carrying our two little inflatable boats – an Avon and a small Zodiac – tied on top of each other.

We couldn't drive through Northern Ireland in a garda van so we had to go the long way around the border and it took us all day to get from the Phoenix Park to Glencolmcille in north-west Donegal. When we arrived there were a few complaints about how long it had taken us to get there, with one of the locals saying that he had come from East Fife in Scotland quicker than us.

The next morning the army had a helicopter flying around the place, and while we were getting ready in the Glen Bay Hotel somebody had the brainwave that myself, Padraig Tunney and John Harrington should be flown to the dive site. As the *Evelyn Marie* had been sister fishing with another boat, the *Summer Star*, its crew had seen the lights go out on the ship when it sank and knew where it had gone down, so the three of us were ushered into a rickety little grey army helicopter and flown to the dive site, three miles out into the ocean, where we were to be, literally, dropped into the sea.

None of us had ever seen a helicopter up close before, let alone jumped out of one, and we were all afraid for our lives. John was to be the first one to jump out and as we hovered a hundred feet above the dive site, he stepped onto the little platform at the edge of the helicopter and gripped the handrail at the side. At the very last minute, however, just as he was about to jump, John had second thoughts and spent a couple of minutes hanging from the helicopter with his legs dangling below him. I could see his knuckles turning white as the army pilot tried to circle in the wind. All the time another soldier was tapping him on the hand and telling him to let go. Eventually, he half fell, half jumped into the crashing waves below.

Although jumping out of a helicopter at that height was a far cry from jumping into Bullock Harbour while training a few months earlier, I tried to remember the same principles and kept one hand clamped over my mask as I shuffled out onto the little ledge. Even though I'd been used to jumping into water from various heights as a youngster, this was a whole different ball game and I was terrified. Somehow I convinced myself that it was the same as leaping off the branch of the tree in the major's or off one of the cranes down the quays in Waterford and I jumped in after John.

When I look back now, it was a crazy thing to have us do. We had no prior experience and were wearing sub-standard clothing and using sub-standard equipment, usually used for leisure diving rather than searching the sea for dead bodies. We were so traumatized by the helicopter jump and the sea was so rough that we ended up being pulled into a boat and brought back to shore shortly after.

Some army divers turned up the next day but despite their officers telling the assembled media that they were 'ready to dive twice a day', none of them had any experience and they never got into the water at all. One of them later confided to me at the hotel bar that they were scared witless and weren't fit to do any diving.

After the helicopter incident, we went out in our own little inflatable a few times, which was probably just as dangerous. Tony 'Oweny' Manus, the skipper of the *Summer Star*, came out with us from Glencolmcille one day to board his own trawler, which was anchored a quarter of a mile out to sea. A seasoned fisherman, Tony was so scared that he knelt down in the inflatable and gripped the two ropes at the side as tightly as he could as we banged up and down in the water on the short journey. Afterwards he swore that he'd never travel with us again.

At the dive site, a boat had dropped a shot line, a rope with a weight at the bottom of it to anchor it down, and we dived down using that for guidance. The sea was so choppy that I lost my torch in the dive but I made my way down along the rope until I came across the wreck of the ship's bow about ninety feet down. Visibility was very bad and the sea crashing against the rocks made the dive extremely dangerous. I was down there for twenty-seven minutes and spent every one of them terrified that I'd get caught up in a net or a rope from the sunken ship in the darkness.

Although we stayed in Glencolmcille for a week or so, the sea was so treacherous that we never dived again. The rest of the crew of the *Evelyn Marie* were never found. It was the first real headline-making fishing disaster in Ireland at the time. Unfortunately, it wouldn't be the last.

# 6

# My first body

Three weeks after the *Evelyn Marie* disaster, the Garda Sub-Aqua Unit was summoned to Tory Island to search for a local woman who had been washed into the sea. The woman, a barmaid in the local pub, had been out walking with her sister, a child and the local priest when a wave came in and dragged her out to sea as she posed for a photograph near some rocks.

Tory Island is nine miles off the top of the Donegal coastline and over 180 miles from our base in Dublin, so – again – it took us almost a day and a half to get our gear ready and drive the two old Bedfords up to the nearest ferry point in Bunbeg. As we made our way across to the island on the local ferry, a helicopter carried our scuba gear over and there was a huge crowd of islanders gathered on the shore when we arrived.

After spending a day and a half travelling up from Dublin and another half a day getting the equipment out to the island, I'd found the body within two minutes. While our diving gear was being spread out on the cliff face I had stuck on a wetsuit, sneaked down to the rocks and jumped into the water to find the body of the missing woman a few feet from the edge of the shore.

Upon seeing the body, I surfaced to tell the others. Living in the Gaeltacht, Tory Islanders have their own language and superstitions steeped in Irish folklore. As soon as they heard me, everyone ran back from the shore like something out of a movie. We put on cylinders and went down and brought the woman's body up to the shore while the helicopter went back to the mainland for a coffin. When the coffin arrived on the island, it was stuffed with about twenty bottles of whiskey and a huge cooked ham. The islanders made salads for us in two of their houses, and after a few strong whiskeys we returned to the mainland and, having completed our first successful recovery, got drunk in the Ostán Na Rosann Hotel in Dungloe.

Although I had recovered my first body from the water for the unit, there hadn't been much skill required. Indeed, we didn't have much skill. Having been trained as sports divers, we had never learned about the methodology of searching underwater and had no idea about search patterns or grids or anything like that. It took some time to figure it out for ourselves.

A few months after Tory Island we were called out to Downpatrick Head near the small town of Ballycastle in County Mayo to search for a missing woman and her three children. Downpatrick Head stands high above the sea and, in the middle of a field running along the cliffs, there is a large square blowhole known as Poll na Sean Tine, or 'hole of the ancient fire', where, on stormy days, the tide rushes in from a subterranean tunnel below and spews out into the field above.

Mary Kate McAndrew was a local woman and was pregnant when she got out of her car, walked up to the blowhole and threw herself and her three young children down into the 126-foot drop to the sea below. When Mary Kate couldn't be found that night, friends and relatives began to panic and searched the area, finding her car near Downpatrick Head the next day. When they looked down into the blowhole they could see her body in the water with one of the children floating beside her.

The local sergeant, Cyril Collins, got a tractor and drove it to the edge of the blowhole, where, after tying a rope around the tractor, he climbed down the inside wall of the hole and somehow managed to get the two bodies up onto land. Sergeant Collins got a Walter Scott Medal for Valor afterwards.

When we arrived, the sea was mashing up through the blowhole and a group of civilian divers gathered near the top warned us that it wasn't safe to go into the water. But when they heard who we were they ran and left their weight belts behind them.

To get to the blowhole, Mick Carr, Padraig Tunney and I had to swim in from the sea. The sea itself was choppy, but when I swam in through the tunnel and into the hole the water was calm and clear. As we swam through, I looked down to see a pair of little red shoes between two rocks and signalled to the lads in the field on the surface that I had one body. It was the seventeen-month-old boy. The others signalled that they had the three-year-old. Having retrieved the little boy's body, I now had to get out of the blowhole without getting mashed up against the rocks on each side. I tried to wait until each rush of water came in so that I could go with the flow on the way out while, all the time, I had this little fella with a lovely head of blond hair tucked under my arm.

When I eventually managed to get out into the sea again, my colleague Jim Brennan was waiting for me on a ledge about four feet up, at the mouth of the tunnel. We had no body bags at the time but Jim got a fertilizer bag from a nearby field and handed it down to me in the water. I put the child into the bag and tried to hand it up to him on the ledge but the bag filled with water and was so heavy Jim couldn't lift it out. I always had a knife strapped to the leg of my wetsuit in case I got caught in ropes or cat gut or anything else, however, so I took it out and cut a hole in the bottom of the bag to let the water drain out.

As the water drained out and the bag got lighter, I handed it up to Jim and a little lock of blond hair flopped out through the hole. It was the first time I had recovered the body of a child and that moment has stayed with me ever since.

As well as the mental strain of searching for missing people, diving is physically demanding and requires a pretty good cardiovascular system, so even though I continued to drink, I tried to stay fit for diving jobs while working on the gate at Garda Headquarters. There was no swimming pool in the park so at lunchtime I would run a three- or four-mile loop around the roads.

There was also a dilapidated gym near the front barrier. All that was in it was an old boxing ring, a few punchbags hanging from the ceiling and a couple of skipping ropes lying on the floor. I completed a boxing coaching course with eleven other gardaí early in the year and we received our certificates from the president of the Irish Amateur Boxing Association, Felix Jones, at the National Stadium. As I still fancied myself as a bit of a slugger, I began to go into the gym during lunch hour and hit the bags every day.

Most of the time there were only two of us in there. Ciaran McGeedy was a sergeant in Crime and Security, also known as the Special Branch. A big strong man of about fifty, he trained the Donegal football team and every day at lunchtime he'd put on gloves and punch the bags. Most days he'd talk me into donning a pair of boxing gloves and then make me spar with him. I was a lot shorter and lighter than him and most days he would beat the shit out of me. If I did manage to get a good wallop at him he'd just get mad and hit me harder.

In the summer of 1975 Garda Dick Conroy, a tailor in the depot and the garda boxing coach at the time, saw me in the gym and asked me to fight in a boxing match during Rialto Festival week. Although I was due to take part in the garda swimming championships the day before, Conroy assured me that I would be fighting a novice boxer and that I would have no problem beating him, so I agreed.

Immediately after the swimming championships I hit May Murray's pub and, without a thought for the fight the next day, stayed there until the early hours. I woke up the next morning with a pounding hangover, but made my way to Rialto, where a makeshift boxing ring was set up in the middle of the surrounding blocks of flats.

Sick from the night before and with the local gougers lining the balconies of the flats, I entered the ring to chants of 'Kill the pig! Kill the pig!' Within seconds of the bell ringing to start the fight, I knew I was in trouble. Hung-over and dehydrated, I was swinging all over the place, while my opponent was landing most of his shots.

In the second round he was cutting the head off me, and the referee, boxer and legendary garda Lugs Branigan, stepped in and stopped the fight, much to the derision of the gougers baying for my blood.

A few minutes later I was leaning on a wall near Kilmainham, vomiting my guts up, when my opponent came over, asked me if I was OK and told me that he had boxed in professional bouts in England.

In September 1975 the crew was called out to Rooskey to search for the body of a Mr Llewellyn, lost off a Shannon cruiser. Having hired a boat from the Emerald Star Line in Carrick-on-Shannon, the man and his family were on a cruise up the Shannon when their young son fell overboard. Although the little lad fell into the water with his life jacket on, his father panicked and dived in to try and save him, getting into difficulty himself. Another boat came along and pulled the boy out of the water – alive – with a boathook, but Mr Llewellyn's body was nowhere to be seen.

The Emerald Star Line gave us a cruiser free of charge to help with the search and we slept in a little bunk each night and ate on the boat to save money.

One of the most important things in any search is to have a witness, to get the location of where the person went into the water. But when you're cruising on the river Shannon for the first time, everywhere looks the same and we spent four days diving in poor visibility, not sure if we were at the right location or not. On the fourth day, just as we were about to give up, we tethered a long metal pole to two ropes tied onto the back of the boat and towed it behind as we all spread out along its length under the water, moving slowly back up the river so that we could scan the area below us. In this way, Pat Tunney found the man's body and we brought him to the shore and awaited an ambulance. When we found him, his trousers were down around his ankles from when he had tried to take them off in panic before diving in after his son.

Susan and her sisters moved to a flat in Glasnevin and we continued to go out at the weekends or whenever I was off duty and she wasn't working. Her new job meant that she would be working on New Year's Eve, so I ushered in 1976 in Waterford with my friends Nicky Power, John Doyle and John Hennessy in the Ard Ri Hotel.

The session came to an abrupt end for me, though, when I fell while dancing and, with my arm out to save myself, landed on one of the many empty pint glasses strewn around the floor and split my right hand open, just under the little finger. The hotel manager called a taxi and I was brought to hospital in nearby Ardkeen, where they stitched my hand up and sent me home. The next day my hand began to swell up and a few days later I noticed that I couldn't move my little finger. I went back to the hospital, where they reopened my hand and took out huge clots of blood from inside the wound. Before they stitched me back up again, they decided to send me for an X-ray, whereupon it was discovered that I had severed a tendon in my little finger.

I was sent to a specialist in Dr Steevens' Hospital opposite Heuston Station, where a Dr Prenderville suggested taking a tendon from my second-last finger and substituting it for the missing one in my little finger. A couple of weeks later I travelled up from Waterford on the train, arriving into Heuston Station at around two o'clock. As I wasn't due into the hospital until five and my surgery wasn't until the next morning, I spent the next few hours in the bar of the Aisling Hotel before checking in.

At half past six on the morning of my scheduled operation one of the patients in an adjacent ward went berserk and broke a window. I went out to help the nurse, but she told me in no uncertain terms to get back into bed as I had 'done enough harm the night before'. I couldn't even remember the night before.

The man in the bed next to me was wrapped in bandages from head to toe and had one of his legs suspended in the air, while one of the hospital decorators, on site to paint the high hospital ceilings, soon joined us when he fell off a scaffold and broke his collarbone after looking down the top of a nurse who had walked underneath. It was like a *Carry On* film.

I ended up in hospital for about ten days after my operation but, unable to stay in bed, I spent most of the time running up and down the halls pushing a young lad in a wheelchair or walking the corridors at night.

My hand injury meant that I would be off work for the next four months and, with little else to do and my wages being sent down to me from Dublin every month, I went on one of the worst benders of my life in Waterford. My friend John Hennessy had taken charge of his father's undertaking business and we began to go everywhere in the Austin Princess he used for funerals. With Nicky and Doyler in tow, we'd go to every horse race within driving distance during the day and then spend our nights playing cards with the bookies. There would be poker games until seven or eight o'clock in the morning after races in Gowran Park, Tramore and even the greyhounds in Clonmel. Although I didn't play cards, I'd sit all night, drinking and watching, and every now and again somebody would send me to the bar to buy another round of drinks and a tray of sandwiches to keep the table going.

John was a very good card player, so good that eventually they wouldn't let him play any more, but for those six months or so he cleaned up. He wouldn't drink when he was playing cards but as soon as the game was over we'd drive to Waterford and he'd make up for it in one of the early houses on the quays.

With his pockets full from the night's winnings, John would start buying drink for everyone, and even on the rare occasion that we went into the pub sober we'd have a sing-song going by eleven in the morning.

Most of the lads I hung around with, both socially in Waterford and in the gardaí, were good drinkers but, unlike me, they never got sick. I could rarely drink without vomiting afterwards. My main problem was that I simply couldn't eat proper food while on a drinking binge. When others would be getting their dinner in the middle of a session, I'd eat almost nothing. I might have the odd bite of a sandwich with the lads at the poker games but I'd never scoff down a plate or two like they would.

If I was drinking after a dive with the unit, I would be so sick the next morning that I would hide in the bathroom of whatever bed and breakfast we were staying in until the rest of the lads were ready to leave. Once breakfast was over and they were ready to go, I'd come down the stairs as the lads were heading out the front door, brushing off the landlady's concern that I'd had no breakfast by telling her I'd slept in and if I didn't go with them I'd be late for work.

While off work for those four months, I'd spend five days a week binge drinking and the other two trying to recover from barely eating for almost a week. Susan would come down to Waterford at the weekends and, having drunk so much during the week, I'd be so sick I couldn't drink any more and my mother would tell her I was off it. But she knew that as soon as she'd gone home I'd be back on the beer again.

I remember waking up one morning at around five o'clock and walking down the town to go into the early house. I then got the bus up the street and went into the Woodman where it was 50p for a brandy. After a while, the girl behind the counter stopped serving me, telling me, 'You're after drinking nearly a bottle there.' I got the bus home, but got off it just 300 yards from my house, where, despite already being full of drink, I went into my local, the Candy Store, where I was only able to take one more drink before walking home.

Although I continued to save a certain amount out of my wages in the Garda Credit Union every week, a lot of my income was spent on drink in that period. I ran out of money at one point and drove out to my friend Mick McGrath, who was working as a petrol pump attendant in a local garage. I gave him a lift home and in return, he filled up my car for free.

In the middle of that bender, things got so bad that I simply had to stop drinking and I took a break for a couple of weeks, which was another habit of mine. If I had something important coming up, I could stop drinking. I could stop and save up for a holiday or get fit for a sporting challenge or before an important or especially risky dive, but, more often than not, if I knew I was going on a big bender in the future, I would stop for a while to give my body a chance to recover for it. But it never took much to persuade me to go back drinking. A wedding, a funeral, a bank holiday weekend or any little excuse and I was away again.

The spell on the wagon ended in a pub in Thomastown. As Doyler and Nicky drank pints after a trip to Gowran Park races, I sipped Lucozade while chatting to John, who was also off the beer in an effort to lose a bit of weight. Midway through the night, though, John tapped me on the shoulder and showed me a newspaper article about heavy people who drank having a longer lifespan. That was enough for us: we both started drinking again.

We made it back to Waterford for a last few drinks. That led to a session in an early house and when I got home, in the middle of the next day, I fell in the door of my parents' house, busting a pane of glass, before staggering through the house to bed. My father followed me and stood in the doorway of the bedroom. 'I think it's time you went back to work.'

# 7

# Two killers come to Ireland

When I finally went back to work towards the end of April 1976 my body was ravaged from the almost four-month-long drinking spree, and after my first day back at work I collapsed in Susan's flat in Glasnevin. Susan remembers me calling her as I watched football on the television, then collapsing on the floor and frothing at the mouth. Not knowing what to do, in an effort to revive me she threw water in my face and I somehow pulled myself to my feet.

I then staggered to the nearest window for some fresh air where, having walked onto the little balcony outside, I ended up falling over the railing and landing in the garden two storeys below. Susan rang an ambulance and when the paramedics arrived and saw me in uniform they rang the guards.

The sergeant who turned up to Susan's flat tried to make out I'd had an epileptic fit and I was brought to hospital in town, where I was kept in for a couple of days. Luckily there were no serious injuries. Although epilepsy was ruled out, one of the doctors there told me to cop myself on, that he had seen 'dockers squeeze more drink out of their shirts' than I was capable of drinking and that I should give it up. To me, though, having epilepsy was a bigger fear than being labelled an alcoholic, as it would have stopped me from diving. I was then admitted to the garda hospital in the Phoenix Park to be assessed before being allowed back on duty a few days later.

Within a few days of returning to the gate I was back diving, this time in the river Liffey, after a woman who had been waiting at a bus stop on Bachelors Walk peered over the wall to see part of a man's torso, including his genitals, lying on one of the steps leading down to the water. The section of torso had been cut just above the waist and just below the genitals and then thrown over the wall – presumably in an attempt to dispose of it in the water – but it had landed two steps higher than the water level at the time. The day after the find we were sent into the Liffey to try and retrieve the other body parts.

As the murder squad went about their work on the surface, we dived around the steps of the Liffey and searched for anything that looked like bones or body parts, bringing everything up to be analysed by the forensic team. During a pretty gruesome few days, we found various bones and bits and pieces of the man's body and also had to bring up the remains of cats and dogs to see if they were human.

While we were diving, Tom Troy, a detective from Store Street, had a hunch that the torso was that of a well-known homeless man from the area. Tom hadn't seen Paddy Hyland wandering the street for a week or so and began to wonder where he was. When this torso came to his attention, Tom was certain it was him. Of course, when Tom told everyone what he thought, the response was invariably to ask how he would recognize the missing man's mickey.

Knowing that Paddy Hyland had been seen with another local man, Tom rang Sean McKeon, who was working as a turner down the docks, to come in for questioning. Much to Tom's surprise, McKeon called to Store Street Station after work and gave a ten-page statement in Irish, confessing to the homeless man's murder.

He had given Hyland a room in his flat, and it emerged that the two men had had a row over alcohol one night and McKeon had beaten Hyland to death with a hammer. Not knowing what to do with the body, McKeon kept it under his bed for three days before deciding to cut it up with a hand saw at his fireplace and put it in plastic bags. He put some of him down the rubbish chute in the flat complex and then on his journey to work every morning would surreptitiously drop one of the bags over the wall of the North Wall Quay and into the river below.

McKeon painted his whole flat afterwards, and when the forensic team searched the premises there wasn't a shred of evidence left. He would never have been caught if it hadn't been for Tom Troy's hunch. Of course, when that hunch was proven correct, the slagging Tom Troy got only intensified.

While sailing back up the Liffey after one of these dives we came across a man and a little girl clinging to an upturned boat in the middle of the river and rescued them. The rescue made the papers the next day and my mother added another clipping to her collection.

*

I had begun to stay more and more often in Susan's flat and, as we had been going out for almost three years, we began to talk about getting a place of our own and even getting married. A week or so after searching for Paddy Hyland, we walked into Murphy and Green's jewellers in town to buy an engagement ring.

There was no grand display of affection or getting down on one knee from me. Susan simply picked out a ring, and on 22 May 1976 we were engaged. Afterwards we went to our favourite restaurant, Captain America's on Grafton Street, for a meal and began to search for a flat together. Shortly afterwards I met a former classmate from Templemore, who persuaded me to play for the garda soccer team. As was my way with everything, I got stuck into training from the off and did nothing by half measures. When I got onto the team I would be the first one at training in the garda grounds in the Phoenix Park and could often be seen hanging two big floodlights off a pole in the pouring rain while the rest of the squad huddled together in their cars, waiting for me to be done so training could start.

Training and playing with the team soon became an excuse for drinking again and, after initially going to the Garda Club in Harrington Street with manager Vinny Hyland and the team after training and matches, I soon started going there on my own most evenings. At the weekends, Susan and Vinny's wife Imelda would join us for a few drinks.

The Garda Club was where everyone changed their cheques at the time and, as there was always a good crowd in the bar, I soon became friendly with guards from other stations and departments. I got to know the lads in the Garda Choir, who were rehearsing for an upcoming three-week trip to America. Soon I was sitting in on their discussions about buying blazers and the booking of their tour of New York and Boston that September. At one of these post-rehearsal chinwags, there was talk of a few free vacant seats on the plane going to America and I was told I could go with them if I had the £99 air fare. Because I was friendly with them, and John Harrington from the diving unit was in the choir, I decided to go.

Towards the end of August, just a few weeks before we were due to leave for New York, I was called to search for a girl who had been reported missing in Wicklow. Elizabeth Plunkett, a twenty-three-year-old from Ringsend in Dublin, had been socializing with some friends in McDaniel's pub near the caravan park in Brittas Bay when she walked out in the rain-lashed night after a bit of a tiff among the group. When she couldn't be found the next day, Elizabeth was reported missing.

A woman in the caravan park had been looking out of her window that morning and saw an old Ford Cortina pulling away from a mobile home that had been broken into overnight. She took the registration number of the car and reported it to the gardaí, who traced it to a criminal in Clonmel. He told local gardaí that he had loaned the Cortina to two Englishmen who had been in Mountjoy Prison in Dublin with him for burglary a few months before.

When the guards checked out the duo – Geoffrey Evans and John Shaw – they found they both had a string of convictions in England and were wanted in connection with three vicious sexual assaults on women in and around Manchester. Evans was a skinny career criminal and Shaw was a powerfully built former coal miner with twenty-six previous convictions including two sex attacks.

Having escaped the clutches of the English law, the pair had arrived in Ireland two years earlier. They began their Irish criminal spree by breaking into houses in the Wicklow area but had been arrested, convicted and sent to Mountjoy. Upon hearing of their conviction in Ireland, British police began extradition proceedings against them and, as part of their court application, sent fingerprints belonging to Evans and Shaw found at the scene of three savage sexual assaults on women in the Manchester area. The extradition hearing in the Bridewell in Dublin, however, deemed the fingerprints insufficient proof for the pair to be shipped back to England, and at the end of their sentence for burglary they were released from custody.

When the local gardaí searched the woods near the caravan park, they found one of Elizabeth's shoes and we were dispatched to Brittas Bay, where we spent most of our time digging sand dunes as we thought she might be buried on the beach somewhere. John Harrington and I both left for New York before the end of the search.

The Garda Choir sang the whole way to America, with me roaring and screaming in the middle of them. When the plane was drunk dry, we opened our duty free and drank that too. While the choir were due to do a concert tour of New York and Boston, I had arranged to stay with my mother's brother Mick Shanahan and his wife Kathy in the Bronx. I was so drunk when the flight landed that by the time he picked me up I could barely see him. I could hear Mick showing me all the sights of New York on the drive to his house but all I could see were blurred lights everywhere.

My mother must have phoned the house to see if I'd made it because I remember hearing my uncle say, 'He's here, but he has a lot of alcohol on board.' The summer heat in the apartment complex was stifling and on that first night I sweated buckets of alcohol. After a few days with the Shanahans, I went to stay with my cousin Cathleen and her husband Tommy in Long Island. Tommy Flaherty was a member of the New York Police Department and he and his partner Howie Berger used to bring me to work with them and show me their beat. Tommy and Howie both worked with Frank Serpico, a local cop who had turned whistle-blower and unveiled a litany of corruption in the NYPD in the late sixties and early seventies. Serpico's story had been turned into a movie three years earlier, with Al Pacino receiving an Oscar nomination for playing the lead role.

That fortnight on the beat in New York opened my eyes to the real dangers of police work and, indeed, to the world at large. Driving down 42nd Street one day, the guys pulled the patrol car up alongside two stunning-looking women, one dressed in yellow and one in red. After a couple of minutes of chit-chat the lads drove off and asked me which one I thought was the best looking. When I answered that both of them looked great, they started laughing and told me that they were two transvestite prostitutes. I was twenty-three years old and had no idea transvestites even existed.

Tommy and Howie let me out of the car at a cinema another day and told me to go watch a movie. Inside, I saw a porn film for the first time ever. When I came back out the guys were waiting, laughing again.

Both Tommy and Howie were always armed and the duo would tell me scary tales of armed robberies, drug trafficking, gang warfare, prostitution and even serial killers as they smoked their way through endless packets of cigarettes.

'Do you have any of that in Ireland, Tosh?'

'No.'

'Well, you will. You'll have all of this and more; the armed robberies, the drug trafficking, the murders, the rapes, and even the serial killers, it'll all come to Ireland eventually.'

After two weeks in New York, I flew from LaGuardia to Boston, without having a clue how I would find the Garda Choir before flying home a few days later. As I walked out with my bags, however, I saw five or six lads in garda blazers standing in the airport terminal, where they had gone to check arrangements for their homeward flight. They gave me a lift back to the digs and told me they'd put me up in a motel with the rest of the choir. When we got to the motel, they put me in a room with a sergeant from Clones – the man who, a couple of years earlier, had warned me about crossing the border to visit Susan. I threw my case on the bed and went into the bathroom to see the bath filled with ice, cans of beer and bottles of whiskey. Every meeting or congregation of any sort was held in that room until we flew home a few days later.

We arrived home to tragic news on two fronts. A young garda, Michael Clerkin from Monaghan, who was just a year older than me, had been killed when a booby-trap bomb went off during a search of a derelict building in Portarlington. Also, the body of Elizabeth Plunkett had been found. She was washed up on the beach at Ballyteigue Bay in Wexford, almost forty miles from where we had been searching in the sand dunes. A lawnmower, stolen from Brittas caravan park, had been tied to her body to weigh her down in the water.

Before the search for Elizabeth Plunkett went nationwide, the chief suspects in her disappearance, Shaw and Evans, were spotted trying to burn clothing in a wood nearby, which aroused the suspicions of local gardaí. The duo gave false names, John and Geoffrey Murphy, but were not arrested and went on their way, only for gardaí to later find one of Elizabeth's sandals and a piece of cardboard with the name Geoffrey Murphy written on it during a search of the woods.

While I'd been away, the search for the duo had gone nationwide and a garda bulletin was put out for the two Englishmen, who made their way to the west of Ireland. Although Evans and Shaw had crudely repainted the Ford Cortina by hand and attempted to change the number plates, a man reported seeing the car at a filling station in Maam Cross in Connemara, but by then they had disappeared again. Shortly afterwards a second girl, Mary Duffy, went missing in Castlebar in County Mayo while waiting for her brother to pick her up from work.

Their eventual capture came after gardaí Jim Boland

and P. J. Corcoran spotted the Cortina outside a hotel while on patrol in Salthill in Galway. They called for backup, keeping watch until Evans and Shaw came out of the hotel disco, and followed them when they drove away. When the pair pulled in along the coast road towards Connemara to let the car behind them pass, the guards stopped in front of them, overpowered them and arrested them without a struggle.

While in custody in Eglinton Street in Galway one of the duo escaped through a window, possibly left open deliberately, and was 'helped' back into the station by a couple of gardaí who were conveniently waiting outside.

Detective Gerry O'Carroll was drafted in from Dublin to help interview the two men. Having arrived late at night from the capital, Gerry had nowhere to stay so he took Shaw out of his station cell at three o'clock in the morning and brought him into a room with a pool table in it to interview him. When Shaw refused to answer his questions, Gerry tried another trick, asking Shaw if he was a Roman Catholic, to which he replied that he was.

'Do you remember your First Holy Communion, John? I bet you your mother was proud of you.'

Seeing this comment hit a raw nerve with Shaw, O'Carroll said, 'Let's say a prayer together, John.'

They were starting the second Hail Mary when Shaw broke down and confessed everything. He made a full statement, admitting both killings and even offering to show O'Carroll the spot in Lough Inagh where they had dumped Mary Duffy's body.

When the duo arrived in Ireland their plan was to

kidnap, rape and murder one Irish woman a week. To fund their scheme they carried out robberies and got caught and sent to jail before they could attack any women. Once released from Mountjoy they were free to put their plan to prey on Irish women into action.

Elizabeth Plunkett was their first victim. Upon seeing her leave the pub in Brittas on that stormy night in August, Evans and Shaw offered her a lift home in the Ford Cortina they had borrowed from their former fellow prisoner. Instead of giving her a lift home, however, they savagely beat her on the way to Castletimon Wood, where they raped her repeatedly.

On the order of Evans, the mastermind of the two psychopaths, Shaw strangled her with the sleeve of a shirt and the duo dumped her body in the woods. That night they stole a boat and threw her into the sea with the stolen lawnmower tied to her body.

Mary Duffy was their second victim. As she waited for her brother to pick her up from work, Shaw attacked her, hitting her with such force that he knocked out her dental fillings, before bundling her into the car. Mary Duffy was beaten, raped repeatedly and very badly injured by the time the car reached Ballynahinch, near Clifden in County Galway.

As they had done with Elizabeth Plunkett, they drove their victim to an isolated wood, tied her to a tree and took turns raping her before they strangled her thirty-six hours later. Once again they stole a boat in the dead of night, this time rowing out onto Lough Inagh and, having weighed her body down with a sledgehammer, an anchor and a concrete block, threw her overboard.

A third victim narrowly escaped with her life after flee-ing from their car just days before the pair were arrested in the wild open countryside of Connemara.

The search for Mary Duffy's body was over when I came back. Lough Inagh is around five miles long and a couple of miles wide and, as the killers had rowed out into the lake in the dark of night, they didn't know where they had dumped the body. With John Harrington and me still in New York with the choir, the navy divers were called in to help the garda divers with the search. The navy brought along thick jackstay ropes, half a mile long. Every day these ropes would be dropped on the bed of the lake, starting at the two outer edges and moving towards the middle as the search went on. A team of divers would search on another rope, in a perpendicular line to the jackstays, for the half-mile length before turning round and searching back up the other side. The jackstays would then be moved to the edge of the previous search and lifted towards each other. This process was repeated every day until the chains met near the middle of the lake. After ten days of diving, there was still no sign of Mary Duffy's body. On the final day, the garda and navy divers were standing on the lakeshore plan-ning their last dive when three civilians pulled up in a car and asked to help. Fobbing them off, Sergeant Bracken told them to go out along the last run of the jackstay. Within five minutes they had found the body.

Immediately, the garda divers entered the water. They removed a wooden door from a nearby hut and put the body on it, with the sledgehammer, anchor and concrete block still attached. As there were no such things as underwater cameras in those days, a helicopter then flew over the site so that the forensic photographer could take pictures of the scene. The divers lifted the body up to the surface and the helicopter came down to take the photos. As the chopper got closer, the rotor blades began to spew bits of dead flesh into the lads' faces and they all began to vomit into the water.

Evans and Shaw were remanded in custody. In 1978 both men were convicted of falsely imprisoning, raping and murdering Mary Duffy and Elizabeth Plunkett and were each sentenced to life imprisonment. They would become Ireland's longest serving prisoners and had gruesomely written their way into the history books as Ireland's first serial killers, or would-be serial killers. Evans died in May 2012, having been in a coma since 2008. Shaw, now in his early seventies, is still alive and in Castlerea Prison.

The murders of Elizabeth Plunkett and Mary Duffy stand among the most horrific ever recorded in Ireland. All too soon, it seemed, the words of the New York cops Tommy and Howie had come true: *The armed robberies, the drug trafficking, the murders, the rapes, and even the serial killers, it'll all come to Ireland eventually.*

# 8

# Working hard and playing hard

After the controversy about how long the Garda Sub-Aqua Unit took to get to the *Evelyn Marie* search, when another Donegal trawler sank in November 1976 new sergeant Paddy Morrissey and I were helicoptered up to search for the missing crew. The *Carraig Una* had left Burtonport on a fishing expedition similar to the *Evelyn Marie* and was lost on the same stretch of rocks around Rathlin O'Beirne Island. Our mission was to locate the bodies of its five-man crew: John Boyle, Michael Coyle, Doalty O'Donnell, Anthony McLaughlin and skipper Ted Carbery.

I spent most of the helicopter flight using karabiner clips, usually reserved for mountaineering, to join ropes in a lasso-type loop so that I could wear them on my belt and use them underwater if necessary. We took wetsuits with us and were given cylinders and a regulator each when we got there. Two students from Belfast, up there diving for the weekend, volunteered to help us search for the missing fishermen.

Rathlin O'Beirne Island is about three miles out in the ocean and we were brought to the dive site in an orange hand-painted boat by a local man, Josey Coyle, and his young son Patrick. We decided to go down in pairs. As we jumped in, we were surrounded by trawlers. These guys knew that nobody had been found in the *Evelyn Marie* disaster twenty-one months earlier and they also knew the terrible conditions. Still, they stood by in the faint hope that we would find the men's bodies.

While the sea was pretty choppy on the surface, the visibility improved as I dived down. Although Paddy had dived in with me, we became separated under the water and a few minutes later I found myself alone on top of a ledge about seventy feet down. I looked around but couldn't see Paddy anywhere so I peered over the underwater ledge to see another big drop below. Although the water overhead was breaking heavily against the side of the island, underneath the ledge was calm and clear so I decided to go deeper.

As I dived under the ledge, I saw the body of a man floating in front of me. He wore a white vest with black trousers but had no socks on, which made me wonder whether he had been in bed when the accident happened. He had suffered a serious eye injury, but instead of getting a fright when I saw him, I was delighted to have found him and swam over on my own and grabbed the body. I tied my makeshift lasso around him and prepared to make my way up to the surface. On the way up it would be crucial to stay away from where the water was smashing against the rocks higher up.

As I began to ascend, Paddy appeared out of nowhere and I gave him the other part of the loop I'd made with the rope. Paddy was a lot older than me and was under a bit of pressure in the rough conditions but one of the

Belfast divers came on the scene too and we kept swimming out away from the rocks. Over our heads I could see the water smashing against the rocks and gave a hand signal to the two lads to keep their eyes open. On the way up, we spotted a lobster pot, used its rope to climb up along and, slowly but surely, we got nearer the top.

As soon as we surfaced I heard somebody shout: 'They're on the surface. I think they have a body.' An RTÉ film unit was making a documentary about the island at the time, and as I got the body into the boat I noticed a trawler coming towards us with the camera crew. Although I was only twenty-three, I was conscious of the fact that the man's family were still to be notified and that there were five grieving families on the shoreline and aboard the other trawlers. I waved at the journalists to go away in the hope that they would have a bit of respect and consideration for the bereaved, but they just carried on filming and put the clip on the news that evening.

The body – identified as that of Ted Carbery – was brought onto the boat, then transferred to one of the trawlers, and the recovery made headlines all over the country. I hadn't realized how much media attention was focused on the disaster after the *Evelyn Marie* tragedy and how much the whole country was watching and waiting for news. The coffin was brought to Burtonport, thirty miles away, while we made our way back to the Glen Bay Hotel in Glencolmcille, where we were treated like heroes.

The local fishermen were delighted with the news because they thought there was a good chance of finding the rest of the crew. But the weather soon worsened and, as the days and weeks went on, it became so bad that, although we went out on boats, walked the island and put out shot lines as often as we could, there were days when some of us just sat around the hotel drinking because we couldn't dive. Three weeks later the search was called off and we returned to Dublin. The body of the *Carraig Una*'s skipper would be the only one ever found by a diver off Rathlin O'Beirne Island.

As I had found his body I was called back up to Dungloe for the inquest into Ted Carbery's death in January 1977. I brought another guard, Ray Sweeney from the transport detail, with me in the hope that he would share the driving duties. Ray had a farm in Letterkenny and, as he worked one week on and one week off, he would travel home to tend the farm every second week. Unfortunately Ray had an awful earache and was unable to drive.

Despite the fact that I was still wearing my garda uniform, I decided to take the direct route to Letterkenny, which meant driving through Northern Ireland. In the middle of the night the car was stopped by British soldiers at a checkpoint in Aughnacloy and we were pulled over to the side of the road.

Immediately, my thoughts raced back to what had happened to the Miami Showband eighteen months earlier. The band had been pulled over at a similar checkpoint by members of the loyalist paramilitary group the UVF, dressed in British army uniforms. They ordered the band members to get out of their minibus and line up by the roadside. Two of the fake soldiers then tried to plant a time bomb in the minibus but the bomb exploded prematurely and killed them both. The remaining gunmen then opened fire on the band members, killing three and wounding the other two. Two gardaí from the Republic would have been prime targets for the UVF and we could easily have met a similar fate.

On seeing we were members of the police force, however, the soldiers brought us into their hut and offered us a hot drink. Although they seemed genuine enough as we drank tea and chatted about our respective duties either side of the border, I still couldn't help but wonder if I could take everything at face value. As I sat there I couldn't help but imagine one of their colleagues planting something in our car while we were being distracted in the hut. Thankfully, though, the checkpoint was real and the soldiers were genuine young lads just trying to break the monotony of their night shift.

I stayed in Ray Sweeney's house that night in Letterkenny and the next morning after breakfast he gave me a bag of spuds for my trouble and sent me across the mountain to Dungloe and the inquest. The inquest was straightforward from my point of view: I simply described what I had seen and done in finding the body. Ted Carbery's brother took me for a drink afterwards, which was the start of a long bender.

As the one who had found the body, I was a hero. Although the local fishermen spent most of their lives at sea, they thought the garda divers were mental for going under the water. I wasn't allowed to put my hand in my pocket in any of the bars around town and as, at the time, pubs in those little fishing villages had a twenty-three-hour licence, the fishermen nearly killed me with alcohol.

The day after the inquest the body of a second *Carraig Una* crew member, John Boyle, was found in a fishing net by one of the local trawlers. After three months in the water, he was only identifiable by his trousers and his belt. I took another couple of days' leave and decided to stay for the funeral, where the fishermen easily persuaded me to help carry the coffin.

Having gone to Dungloe for just one day, I had now been gone three and Susan was sitting in her flat in Glasnevin trying to figure out how to contact me when she switched on the six o'clock news on RTÉ to see me coming down the steps of the church carrying the coffin of the missing fisherman.

She now knew roughly where I was but it took her another two days to track me down to where I was staying. In a pub, naturally.

'Are you coming home, or what?'

After promising her I was on the way home, I went to Sunday Mass in Dungloe and stood at the back of the chapel, dying with a hangover. Afterwards, I went back to the Crib pub to collect my bag, drank three bottles of Harp lager, got into my car and took off for Dublin.

It was a full day's drive, interrupted only by a long delay at another army checkpoint in Aughnacloy (this one following the killing of local GAA member Aidan McAnespie by a soldier the day before), and stops either to urinate or to vomit from my hangover, before I made it to

Glasnevin that night. When I got to the door of the flat, Susan and her sisters were going down to the local for a drink so, naturally, I joined them. I spent most of the night vomiting green bile into the men's toilets.

Two months after Ted Carbery's inquest I was called back up to Donegal, this time to Cashelard outside Ballyshannon, where a seven-year-old girl, Mary Boyle, had gone missing on St Patrick's Day.

The Boyle family was visiting Mary's grandparents' remote cottage in Cashelard when, just before dinner, Mary, dressed in trousers and a knitted cardigan and with her long hair tied back with a ribbon, went outside to play with her twin sister, Ann, and her older cousins. At around 3.45 p.m. Mary's uncle, Gerry Gallagher, who had been working on the roof of his house, decided to return a borrowed ladder to his neighbours, the Cawleys, who lived across the bog 400 yards away.

Mary munched on a bag of Tayto crisps as she trailed behind her uncle towards the Cawleys' house but when she reached a water-filled patch of bog, he told her to turn back. Her uncle chatted briefly with the Cawleys and returned to the house at 4.30 p.m., when it was discovered that Mary hadn't made the five-minute trek home and was missing.

Although Mary Boyle disappeared on 17 March, it took a while for us to be called to the scene and I did my first dive in Lough Unshin, at the back of her grandparents' house, on 6 April. A trench was later dug by a mechanical digger and the entire lake was drained but it produced no body.

We then dived in Colmcille Lough, a couple of miles away, which had been used as a reservoir so the water was very clear. I swam over and back on a rope moved by men on the surface, but all I could see were broken bottles, rocks and a few eels. As there was no boat in the area, we only covered the edges of the lake. We also walked the bogland and dived in bog holes, where we thought she might have been swallowed up by the marshy ground.

After two weeks of painstaking searches across the bog, no body was found and the case of Mary Boyle's disappearance has never been solved.

When Mary's mother had looked out the front door and discovered her daughter wasn't playing with the other children in the front garden, her brother Gerry was fixing a stone wall in front of the house. When she asked if he had seen Mary, he didn't answer, so she'd thought he hadn't heard her.

Ten minutes later, when she asked again if anyone had seen Mary, Gerry Gallagher drove off in his car. When he came back to the house he said that Mary had followed him earlier to the Cawleys' house before turning back.

On the day of her disappearance, there were three brothers poaching from the lakeshore, the postman was doing his rounds in a white van, while another van was also seen in the area. A man cutting timber across the road said he saw a white van go past but thought it was the postman. A girl standing at Cashelard graveyard with her father and a local man saw a white van come flying round the corner and said that the man driving the van had a priest's collar on him, remarking that he looked like 'the kind of priest you wouldn't visit'.

Years later, it was discovered that Robert Black, the most notorious British paedophile of all time, with nine murders of children to his name and the chief suspect in numerous other unsolved cases, was in the area at the time. Gardaí know now that Black was in Ballyshannon, just five miles away, on the day Mary Boyle went missing. Black claims to have killed at least nineteen girls across the Continent but he has never mentioned Mary Boyle in any of his interviews.

On 14 May 1977 a British intelligence officer, Robert Nairac, who had been posing as an IRA man from Belfast, was abducted from outside the Three Steps pub in Dromintee, South Armagh. Calling himself Danny McErlaine and saying he was from the Ardoyne, Nairac even sang a rebel song, 'The Broad Black Brimmer', with the band on stage that night. Afterwards he was set upon by four members of the IRA in the car park. Nairac, a former boxer, did not go down easily and, having given as good as he got, he made a dash for his red Triumph Toledo and the 9mm Browning pistol that was stashed inside.

Two of his attackers hauled him back, however, and he was knocked unconscious, bundled into a waiting car and driven across the border to a field near Ravensdale Woods, where he was set upon again, this time by a group of nine men. Two days later the IRA announced that, having confessed to being an SAS man, Nairac had been executed.

The Garda Sub-Aqua Unit was brought in to help with the search for his body.

After searching the rivers and quarries in the area, our unit also helped out with the land searches and we spent four days combing the fields and finding various pieces of evidence. I found lots of coins all around the field and when the forensic team put their marker flags down you could see the pattern where Nairac had literally been beaten around the field. We also found a piece of his jaw-bone in a corner. A bullet was found in the ground where he had been shot in head, while the gun used to shoot him was also found, hidden in a wall.

With no body to be seen, though, we were given a tip-off that Nairac had been dumped into a meat grinder at the nearby Ravensdale Meats factory and churned up with all the blood and bones of the slaughtered cattle. With an old orange overall over my wetsuit, I spent a few hours search-ing inside the huge tanks as a mixer churned the blood, guts and bones all around me. Robert Nairac's body was never found.

Six months later Liam Townson, a twenty-four-year-old IRA member from Meigh village, just outside Newry, became the first man in Ireland to be convicted of murder without the victim's body being found. After he confessed to the killing and implicated other members of the IRA gang involved, the story of Nairac's struggle with his cap-tors was eventually pieced together.

Despite being punched, kicked and pistol-whipped around the Ravensdale field, Nairac would not reveal his true identity to his captors. Townson, the local IRA commander at the time, was called and arrived at around 2 a.m. after picking up the handgun from its hiding place in the wall. Even though he was now faced with certain death, Nairac protested his innocence, and, unsure as to whether he was telling the truth, an armed Townson marched his battered and bloodied captive to a corner of the field so that he could interrogate him on his own.

Although he had been battered around the field and was badly injured, Nairac somehow managed to overpower Townson and get the gun off him. When he pulled the trigger to shoot his captor, though, the gun jammed and he was knocked to the ground by a blow to the face with a paling post by one of the others, which is when he lost the bit of jawbone that we found.

With Nairac, who was a Catholic, lying face down in the grass, a last effort to elicit information from him was made when one of the gang knelt beside him and, pretending he was a priest, asked to hear his confession before administering the last rites. When the British soldier refused, Townson put the gun to Nairac's head and, after it misfired twice more, shot him dead on the third attempt.

In early 1977, Susan and I were both miles away from our parents and nobody in the area knew whether we were married or not, so we moved into a flat together on Dublin's North Circular Road and began to look for our first house.

A few months later we were shown a three-bedroom semi-detached show house in a new housing estate in Blanchardstown and innocently believed the salesman when he told us there would be no other houses ever built in the area. We scraped together the money for the deposit and were approved for a mortgage to buy the house, which cost £10,595. We left the solicitors, having signed for the house, and didn't have the price of a meal that evening. Shortly after, we got the keys and moved into our first real home.

As we had very little money to furnish the place, we had to improvise. We managed to buy a washing machine, a fridge-freezer and an oven with the last of our savings but had nothing left for other luxuries, so the concrete floors downstairs and the chipboard floors upstairs remained bare for a long time. My parents came up from Waterford to help us settle in and my father's gardening skills were soon put to good use digging rocks and lumps of concrete blocks out of the soil in the back garden.

We didn't have much in financial terms but we had a new home and, with a wedding planned for the following year, all we wanted then was to be together. Susan continued to work while I could be called away on searches in various parts of the country at any time. When I wasn't away, I still spent a lot of my spare time drinking in the garda canteen at headquarters, or in the Garda Club in Harrington Street, and Susan spent a lot of her time on the phone trying to chase me down and get me home.

Having gone to the Garda Club to watch Dublin beat Armagh in the All-Ireland Final in September that year, I spent most of the day drinking with colleagues before hopping into my new Ford Cortina and drunkenly driving home. While cutting through the Phoenix Park I hit a bullock that had strayed out onto the road and wrecked my third car in almost as many years. The dead bullock was found near Áras an Uachtaráin the next morning and I ended up having to pay compensation to its owner.

# 9

# A wedding to remember

After being pretty active in our first two years of existence, a row over budgets put a halt to the Sub-Aqua Unit's gallop in early 1978. While we were attached to the Defence Unit in Garda HQ the barracks master, who was a chief superintendent, was deemed to be in charge of us and paid our wages. But after a while, whenever we were called out to a search that required a few days away, he maintained that the superintendent in the Garda HQ garage was then responsible for us and that whatever overtime and subsistence expenses were incurred had to come out of his budget. The upshot of the infighting was that we ended up being tied to headquarters for long periods, and dives were few and far between.

In April, however, we were asked to search the Liffey for a garda who had been reported missing. After his car had been found on the docks near Burgh Quay, with the keys still in the ignition, it was feared that the garda had committed suicide. In our first search that morning, I dived with John Harrington while Paddy Morrissey sat in a small boat in the middle of the river alongside Mick Carr, the duo acting as cover in case we found the body.

As we were searching, I came across a blue ladies' bike under the water. Even though it could have been in there for years, the bike looked in decent condition to me, so I tied a rope around it and pulled it out. I leaned the bike up against the riverside wall before continuing with the rest of my dive. Although the visibility was reasonably good in that part of the Liffey, we got out of the water for lunch without having found the body.

I went down to the bathrooms in nearby Pearse Street garda station during lunch break and, having had a shower, was standing naked in the middle of the floor when the local superintendent walked in.

'You can finish up that diving now this evening,' he said. 'That'll be it now, no more after today.'

I knew there had been discussions about cutbacks and arguments about who was to pay us while we dived, but we were now looking for one of our own, and I was outraged that we were going to be sent home after such a short search period.

'For fuck's sake!' I roared. 'We're out diving for gougers and criminals for weeks and when we're looking for a guard we're sent home after a day. What's going on?'

'Don't mind that, just finish up that diving today.'

I was disgusted with the decision to send us home after a day. What I didn't know was that since morning the superintendent had found out that the 'missing' garda had actually run away with a young girl from down the country.

Without any idea that we were searching for nothing, after lunch we swapped roles and Mick Carr and Paddy

Morrissey got into the water while I sat in the little boat alongside John as cover for the two divers. By now, a decent-sized crowd had gathered at the side of the road to peer in at us, while the superintendent stood, hands in his pockets, watching us from the bank and telling us to hurry it up.

Suddenly, Mick and Paddy surfaced with the body of a man a few yards down the river. The superintendent took one look at the dead man's blue overalls and shouted down to me in the boat.

'They're not guard's clothes!'

I was disgusted and, in an attempt to wind him up, stood up in the middle of the boat and waved to Mick and Paddy in the water and shouted to them at the top of my voice.

'Lads, that's the wrong fella! Fuck him back in!'

With the crowd looking on, the super began to get flustered and didn't know what to say as we pulled the body on board.

We brought the body in and laid him out along the steps near the wall. We still had no body bags, but somebody managed to get some polythene sheeting from a building site across the road and we wrapped him up in that. We used a bit of the rope that we had been searching with to tie the polythene around the man's legs and waist in an effort to keep the body covered, but were apprehensive about doing this because we knew we'd have a hard time begging for another bit of rope from the garda stores when we went back. It seems ridiculous but that's the sort of stuff we were worried about then – not having a bit of rope to be able to do the next search.

After a few minutes, a little Dubliner in his fifties came waddling past the scene, pulling on a cigarette. In the rest of the country people would often come over to offer a bit of help or to say a prayer if they saw you pull a body out of the water, but diving in the centre of Dublin was always different.

'How's it goin'?' said the man in a thick Dublin accent as he went past. He took another drag on his cigarette and looked down at the body on the ground for a few seconds before wandering over to the bike leaning up against the wall after the first dive. He gave the bike a quick once-over before turning round, waddling past the dead body again and back over to me.

'Good enough for him,' he said, nodding towards the body in the polythene sheeting. 'No bleedin' brakes!'

The body turned out to be that of a missing Welsh sailor, who had fallen overboard three weeks earlier. Apparently, a Dublin Port and Docks diver, employed to repair ships in the docks and with no experience in searching for bodies, had gone down to look for him when it happened. We had never even been told the man was missing.

I threw the ladies' bike into the back of our van and brought it back up to HQ, where I hosed it down, cleaned it off and plastered it with oil. A few evenings later I was having my usual post-patrol drink in the garda canteen in the park when another guard, Mick Ryan, began telling the assembled crew how his wife was trying to lose a bit of weight and do a bit more exercise.

'I've the very solution for that, Mick. I've a nice little ladies' bike that I'll sell to you.'

TOSH

I brought Mick over to a hut at the back of the gate where the bike was parked under a canopy and showed it to him.

'That's a top-class bike, Mick. A ladies' bike.'

Mick gave me a tenner for the bike and we went back into the canteen and drank the proceeds between us.

A couple of months later Mick arrived into the canteen after work.

'Jaysus, Tosh, that bike you sold me fell asunder. I brought it into the bike shop the other day and the fella told me that all the ball bearings, the wheels, the spokes . . . everything is rotten.'

I didn't feel it was the right time to divulge to Mick that the bike had been at the bottom of the Liffey for maybe two years prior to his wife taking it for a spin. Instead, I reminded him that we had drunk the money for the bike anyway and there was never another word about it.

With a wedding coming up in July and little diving to be done, the only way to boost my overtime was to do security at Portlaoise Prison on my days off. Portlaoise was the only high-security prison in Ireland, and had had an influx of IRA and subversive prisoners owing to the Troubles. After numerous escape attempts – including one where nineteen IRA prisoners blew a hole in the prison wall with explosives in broad daylight – extra gardaí and armed soldiers were deployed to the prison to act as a deterrent.

As there were very few spare gardaí in any of the stations, the only way they could get guards to do security duty in Portlaoise was on their days off, which meant you were getting paid time and a half midweek and double time if you were lucky enough to be sent there on Sunday. Every morning, about fifteen Bedford minibuses would pull up outside the garda depot in the park and, after a quick parade, we would be lined up and a dozen guards would hop into each minibus to begin the journey down. With the time it took to get to and from Portlaoise also included in your overtime, it was no wonder the prison soon became nicknamed 'the mines' by grateful gardaí.

In July, Susan cleared out the wardrobes and tidied up our new house in Blanchardstown in anticipation of some of her family staying over for a day or two before our wedding at the end of the month.

One last trip to Derrylin as singles saw us stay with Susan's parents on the Wednesday before the wedding and, while Susan got stuck into some last-minute wedding arrangements, I met up with a few former colleagues and some of the people I had got to know during my twenty-two months' service in nearby Ballyconnell and we spent the night in one of the local pubs.

The following afternoon we packed the boot of my Ford Cortina with wedding presents (the car had been repaired after the incident with the bullock in the Phoenix Park a few months earlier). Susan's sister Geraldine and her two young brothers Marty and Seán hopped into the back seat and we headed for Dublin, where my stag was due to take place that night.

Still hung-over from the night before, I wasn't paying proper attention to the road and somewhere in between Virginia and Kells the car left the road, flipped over a ditch and landed on its roof in a field. Somehow I came away unscathed, as did the back-seat passengers, but Susan was in pretty bad shape with a broken collarbone and three fingers on her right hand torn open and also broken.

As we clambered out of the upside-down car, Garda Pat Kelly, who had been stationed with me in Ballyconnell, came on the scene and called an ambulance. Susan and the others were carted off to hospital in Navan, Pat put the wedding presents in his car to keep for us until after the wedding and he gave me a lift into Virginia.

Here, I went into a pub and drank a rum and blackcurrant for the first time in my life and, as I sat at the bar, I tried to figure out how I was going to get to Dublin in time for my stag. Pat gave me a lift to Navan Hospital, where I found that Susan was being kept in, so I called a friend to pick me up and bring me to Dublin for my stag. I finally arrived – late – at Pat Culhane's pub outside the Special Criminal Court to find the lads from the soccer team and from HQ already well on.

The next morning, despite being in terrible pain, Susan signed herself out of hospital to get ready for the wedding the following day. As her family were from Fermanagh and mine were from Waterford we had decided to get married in Blanchardstown in an effort to meet halfway. With Susan's family using our house as their base for the wedding, I left to stay with her uncle in Drumcondra. Even though I was getting married the next morning, I brought her uncle out for a drink that night and we ended up in the Chinaman pub near Dublin Castle, a well-known after-hours drinking haunt for the guards at the time.

Despite feeling a bit the worse for wear the next morning, I got up early and dressed in my wedding suit – a blue velvet coat and black trousers – and made my way to Garda Headquarters, where my old Waterford friends John Hennessy and Nicky Power were to pick me up in John's Austin Princess and bring me to the wedding. The lads drove me to the church in Blanchardstown and left me standing outside on my own while they headed for the nearest pub. As I paced up and down outside the front of the church, I began to wonder if anybody was coming to the wedding at all and, with a parched mouth and throbbing headache, was tempted to join them in the pub for a cure.

In due course the guests arrived and, although I was still dying for a drink, I was soon standing at the altar watching my wife-to-be walk up the aisle with her arm in a sling. The ceremony itself took my mind off my hangover a bit, at least until it came to giving out Communion. When the priest handed me the chalice of wine, I began to gulp it down and only stopped drinking when he leaned over and said, 'Leave some for the bride!'

After the ceremony, we stopped the Austin Princess for photos at the monument in the Phoenix Park and outside Áras an Uachtaráin before making our way to the Garda Club, where the reception cost us £500 for around 200 guests. Although I was now sick from my drinking the night before, I tried to man up and eat my dinner and the reception went really well.

We were supposed to go to Spain on honeymoon but because of Susan's injuries we ended up going to London to stay with relatives for a few days instead. My brother and best man, Philip, and his wife came with us. After the bender I'd been on in the run-up to the wedding it took me about three days in England to recover. As soon as I did, I started drinking again.

# 10

# Disaster in Bantry Bay

On 8 January 1979, Ireland awoke to horrific news of its biggest ever maritime disaster. A French-registered oil tanker, the *Betelgeuse*, had exploded in the early hours of the morning while discharging its cargo at the offshore jetty of the Whiddy Island oil terminal off Bantry Bay. Having discharged 74,000 tonnes of heavy crude oil, the ship was unloading another 40,000 tonnes of light crude when the explosion happened, splitting the 924-foot vessel in half and setting the surrounding sea on fire.

The force of the explosion blew people into the water from the jetty that ran alongside the huge ship. Months earlier a bridge that had connected the jetty to the mainland had been removed to make room to berth another ship. So there was no escape from either the ship or the jetty. Within minutes the *Betelgeuse* was engulfed in a ball of flames. About twelve hours after the explosion, the centre of the *Betelgeuse* sank, leaving both ends of the massive ship sticking up out of the water and its cargo of oil pouring into the ocean.

Firefighters called in from Bantry were unable to get near the vessel because of the intense heat. Afterwards it was reputed to have reached 1,000 degrees Celsius and it dissolved eighteen inches of concrete from the walls of the jetty, with half of its 1,000-foot length crumbling into the sea. The firefighters managed to prevent the fire from spreading to the massive oil storage tanks on the island and then tried to contain the spread of flames in the sea.

Shortly after hearing the news of the explosion we were called out and, having mustered as many divers as we could, the Sub-Aqua Unit was on the way to the incident in its clapped-out Bedfords. The local hotel was full of French people from the two oil companies, Total and Gulf, and there were no rooms left for us. The manager took us to the back of the hotel and gave us compact little bunks in the staff quarters. We stayed there for the duration of the search.

On arrival in Bantry a local diver who owned a dive shop was wheeled out to give us advice about the area, but he had no knowledge of searching for bodies at all, and when we went to the dive site the next day it soon became apparent that we were totally unprepared for the scale of the task ahead of us.

A Dutch company, L. Smit and Co., had been charged with salvaging the ship for its owners. While the Dutch divers busied themselves getting ready to recoup the oil companies' losses, a few hundred yards away we were getting ready to dive into an oil slick to search for lost souls. The contrast between us was striking. The Dutch had arrived with equipment we garda divers could only dream of. First, at the most basic level, they had drysuits. We used our wetsuits all year round, even in snow and ice. (Some of the lads resorted to pissing in their suits to try and keep warm during the winter but I had been warned that this would rot my suit so I never did it.) Based aboard their own ship, the *Barracuda*, just off the mainland, the Dutch salvage squad had two massive cranes on floats for lifting the sunken vessel off the seabed, as well as the most up-to-date underwater equipment available at the time. They had video cameras and a communications system so they were able to talk to each other as they cut and welded the hull of the ship underwater. They used a surface-demand air supply, which meant that they wore a helmet with an unlimited supply of air continuously pumped down to them through a hose, known as an 'umbilical', from the surface. They also had a three-way failsafe air system that switched onto an air bank if the compressor supplying the air to the umbilical on the surface broke down, and if they were unlucky enough for that to fail they also carried a small emergency cylinder, known as a 'bail-out bottle'. They could be down there for hours.

Although the TV comedy *Father Ted* was yet to be created, the Garda Sub-Aqua Unit could have provided inspiration for its writers if they had seen us on that first day in Whiddy, dressed in our do-it-yourself wetsuits, with masks on our heads barely fit for the local swimming pool and carrying a nine-foot inflatable dinghy wrapped in cloth under our arms.

When they saw our sub-standard equipment, the oil company offered to buy us new gear but Sergeant Morrissey wouldn't let them so we set off in our little blow-up dinghy with a forty-horsepower engine on the back of it.

On our first day, we were brought out to the island,

where the huge oil reservoirs were sited, and given a shed for our stuff. As we got out of the boat we were greeted by a big steel sign proclaiming the number of accident-free days at Whiddy. Somebody had crossed it out and written '50 dead' in thick black marker.

We were told we could use whatever we wanted from the oil company's stores so immediately I went in and got five reels of rope. I was reprimanded by Sergeant Morrissey for getting too much but I knew it would have taken me ten years to get it in Garda Headquarters.

Using scuba gear, each of us garda divers had a 200-bar cylinder of air. The last 50 bar of that was our reserve air and was activated by pulling a little wire on our cylinders, which meant that we had about thirty-five minutes in the water before we had to surface. If any of us got caught up in ropes, trapped under part of the ship, or simply stayed too long underwater and used up the last few bar of air, there was nothing else left. We would drown.

For our first dive we agreed to go down along the concrete poles that supported the jetty alongside the ship, to get the feel of the conditions below the surface. I jumped out of the dinghy with Donal Gibbons and, as we sank down into the ocean, which was chilled by an icy January breeze, the water colour went from black at the top to green a few metres below and then got blacker and blacker until you couldn't see anything at all. When we got about a quarter of the way down, at around thirty feet, Donal squeezed my arm and we stopped. I knew he wasn't happy and didn't want to go any further, so we stayed at the same depth for a while and simply pretended we had gone all the way down to the bottom when we surfaced.

When we got out, everyone agreed that the conditions were atrocious, the worst we'd ever seen. Donal confided in me that he wouldn't be diving there any more and, true to his word, he stayed in the boat on the surface for the rest of our time in Whiddy.

We were caked in oil from head to toe. Afterwards we found some oil-removing soap used by the workers at the terminal and washed in it before mixing it with water and power-hosing our wetsuits down in an effort to clean the oily gunk off them.

At the end of the jetty there was a platform called Dolphin 22. The terminal workers were ferried to and from Dolphin 22 every day as they went about loading and unloading the ships. It had a phone box from which they would ring the skipper of the launch boat when they wanted to be collected. Crew members of visiting foreign tankers used it to phone home.

When the *Betelgeuse* exploded, those who weren't blown into the water ran towards the phone booth, presumably out of instinct, to call for help, but the wind blew the flames towards them and the sea eventually got them too. If they had run in the other direction, where the other end of the jetty remained undamaged, they would likely have been saved.

As we knew the workers had congregated around that spot, we concentrated our search efforts around that end of Dolphin 22 for the next few days and dropped a

weighted shot line down along one of the support col-
umns at the end of the platform. The plan was that we
would dive down using the shot line for guidance before
tying another rope to the weight at the bottom and branch-
ing off that to search along the seabed for bodies.

The day after our test dive, on 15 January, I jumped in
with John Harrington and, with our wetsuits covered in
plastic overalls in another *Father Ted* effort to protect them
from the oil, we began to work our way down along the
shot line on our first search dive. Although I still couldn't
see anything with the oil and gunk on the seabed, I was
trying to feel around in the darkness to tie the search rope
around the weight when I came across something a few
inches away from the bottom of the shot line.

I felt around another bit in the oily water and, although
there was absolutely no visibility, I knew when I lifted the
object that it wasn't concrete so I felt around a bit more
and realized it was a body. My mind was racing as I grabbed
the body, tucked it under my arm and slowly headed back
up along the shot line towards the surface. I knew there
was huge media attention on the disaster and for me to
find the first body on the seabed was a big deal, so I was
elated.

As I got nearer the surface the visibility got slightly better. I shone my torch under my arm to see an oil-covered
burnt-out skull with teeth protruding from it. As I shone
the torch around, I soon realized I didn't have a full body
under my arm.

The explosion had blown off all of his limbs apart from
one arm, while the fire had charred the rest of his body.

Being told to surface slowly in case you got the bends is all right in theory. In practice, when looking into the murky, dark water and seeing half a dead body with a burnt-out skull and teeth looking up at you, it's very hard not to panic.

Although I wanted to get to the surface as quickly as possible and get rid of him, I knew I had to be careful and I made a couple of decompression stops near the top, John staying with me to the surface. That evening in the hotel, we were feted as heroes again and, as usual, a few drinks were bought for the men who had recovered a body.

The next day Jim Brennan and Mick Carr located a second body under the water but, owing to its location and the amount of debris surrounding it, they couldn't recover it. John and I went down after them but couldn't find it, as we swam in the wrong direction when we got to the end of the shot line. Jim and Mick recovered their body later on. John and I went back down in the afternoon and found another male with one arm. He was eventually identified by his wedding ring.

Diving was halted for the next few days as the noxious fumes from the fire hung in the air and we were unable to fill our air cylinders because of the pollution. Indeed, massive plumes of black smoke stayed billowing into the west Cork skies for days after the accident. The Dutch salvage ship had an air bank on board that could fill ten divers' cylinders in ten minutes, but the Garda Sub-Aqua Unit had to use compressors – like those used to inflate tyres in a garage – to fill ours. Attached to a generator, which was started by pulling a string like a lawnmower starter, it would take half an hour for us to fill one cylinder. We went through a few weeks of this before somebody finally copped that the fire brigade also filled the cylinders for their breathing apparatus using an air bank and if we got an adapter for the air connection on our cylinder heads we could go to any fire station and fill our cylinders in minutes.

Bantry Bay had been picked by Gulf Oil for its depth and, as we were diving in over 120 feet of water, there was always the chance that one of us could get the bends. At the time, Johnny Butler from Dunmore East, a shipwright with some commercial diving equipment, was one of the few people in Ireland who had a private decompression chamber, and after a few days he transported it to Whiddy Island in case of emergency.

We had mainly been used to diving in shallower waters and had no experience of using a decompression chamber; of course, the Dutch salvage crew had their own chamber on board their ship. By now, navy divers had been called in to help us and they, like the Dutch crew, had surface-demand diving gear and had also been trained in using decompression chambers at their headquarters in Cobh.

The decompression chamber was like a big cylindrical Portakabin and consisted of two sealed compartments where the air pressure could be adjusted to mimic the effects of being underwater. Having been artificially brought back down to the same atmospheric level the diver was at in the water, the air pressure would be slowly adjusted by somebody on the outside so that the bubbles in his bloodstream that caused the bends or other illness could be released safely. Just like being underwater, if the pressure went down too quickly inside the chamber, it could kill whoever was in there.

The main chamber had a couple of beds in it so that a diver who resurfaced from a deep dive too quickly could stay there and be treated for days if necessary. The smaller sealed chamber ran outside the front of the bigger one like a hall and you had to be locked in there first before going into the second. It was also used to take in food or by lads swapping over to stay with the patient for a while. The chamber was used once in Whiddy for the officer in charge of the navy divers, Dan O'Neill, for a few hours after he became unwell following a dive. A doctor was locked inside with him while one of the Dutch lads adjusted the pressure from the outside.

As we were using basic scuba gear, the garda divers always tried to stay within the allotted dive-depth tables so that we didn't have to decompress much on the way up. We used a depth gauge on our arm with an arrow on it that would tell you if you were in decompression but in Whiddy I could never see mine with the oil in the water. On the way to the surface on every dive, I always did a safety stop for three or four minutes about twenty feet from the top to de-gas and then again for a couple of minutes within ten feet of the surface.

Although I didn't really need the decompression chamber after diving in Whiddy, I found another good reason for visiting it some mornings on the days we weren't allowed to dive because of the gas in the air. In the main decompression chamber there were oxygen masks hanging down by the beds and the odd morning after spending the night in the Spanish Tavern I went into it, strapped on an oxygen mask, lay down and had a bit of a nap to clear my hangover. Having said that, because of the dangerous conditions, I usually limited myself to four or five pints if we were diving the next day.

Most nights after dinner we'd go down to the Spanish Tavern in Bantry. In the pub, we'd meet up with the Dutch divers, who nicknamed us the 'lake-a-pickers' upon hearing how we had recovered two bodies. They didn't want to see any bodies; they were simply there to salvage stuff for the oil companies and, having seen us dive with such shitty equipment, they couldn't make up their minds whether we were the bravest or the stupidest people they had ever met.

At the weekends John Harrington lent me his car and I drove across the country to Waterford to meet Susan, who would come down from Dublin on the train, and we would stay in my mother's house. Susan would go home on the last train on Sunday night while I would get up early on the Monday morning to race the 125 miles to Bantry and get the half-nine boat out to Whiddy.

With the *Betelgeuse* almost snapped in half under the water, the Dutch crew got a huge chain and tied it to two tugs each side of the wreck. By moving the boats back and forth in opposite directions, they split the wreck in half, then began filling the front portion with foam so that they could float it out to sea and scuttle it.

When naval officer Dan O'Neill was out of action, I got a loan of his torch for my next search, on 22 January, and couldn't believe its power when I turned it on. By comparison, the garda torch I had been using was like a candle. I was so impressed that I wrote the make of the torch in my log book afterwards.

Having gone down the shot line again, John and I swam out along the search rope as he shone his torch to the left and I shone mine to the right. A few yards away my new torch picked up the shell of a life raft over to my right. It was the only thing that stood out, as it was white in the darkness, but as we were trying to keep a system in place for searching we stayed on the search rope on the way out.

On the way back up we went over to the shell and searched around it to find a hand sticking up from the sea-bed, buried in rubble. We were coming towards the end of our dive, however, so we were wary of using up all our air trying to dig out the body and then not having enough time to get to the surface. We tied the search rope to a length of half-buried steel nearby so that we could easily find the body the next morning.

That evening John and I were having our dinner and a few drinks in the West Lodge Hotel when the nine o'clock news came on the hotel television.

'Garda divers have located another body in Whiddy Island today and will attempt to bring it to the surface tomorrow.'

As the night wore on and more drinks were had, John and I began to get paranoid about whether we had actually found a body at all. There were people from all over the world staying in the hotel, most of them waiting on news of a relation missing in the disaster, and the more we drank, the more worried we got.

The next morning two navy divers said they'd come with us to help but they were so inexperienced at searching for bodies that they decided to bring a stretcher and a body bag down with them, thinking that they would be able to put the body into the bag at the bottom of the sea and then carry it to the surface on the stretcher.

Keen to get to the body before the navy lads, John and I lashed down ahead of them and as soon as we touched the bottom I took off towards where I thought the body was. Even though our descent had disturbed all the silt and oil and we couldn't see anything, I made my way along the guide rope to the lump of steel and found the life-raft shell and then the hand sticking out of the seabed. I threw the shell to one side before scrambling in the dark to clear the rubble covering the body and, with it tucked under my arm before the navy lads got to us, I signalled for everyone to go back up. Delighted that I had the body under my arm, I knew I could take my time and went up the line nice and steady. The navy lads gave us a hand getting the body into their body bag on the surface and putting it into our inflatable dinghy before transferring it to a bigger boat a few yards away.

Having found a third body for the garda unit, I got out of the water elated but mentally exhausted. After throwing off my gear on the shore, I was met by Vincent Flood from the Garda Technical Bureau, who congratulated me and politely told me to wash myself thoroughly to make sure I didn't get any disease from the body I'd just brought up, to which I replied, 'If you don't get me a bowl of soup and a sandwich, I'll get frozen to death!'

Vincent ran off immediately and minutes later came out with a bowl of soup.

Once again, having brought up a body, it was time to celebrate and a few drinks were had in the hotel that evening and at the Spanish Tavern that night, where one of the Dutch salvage crew turned to me at the bar.

'Hey, lake-a-picker, you get big allowance for your work?'

'One fifty a day,' I said.

'One hundred and fifty a day? This is good, no?'

'Not one hundred and fifty. One pound fifty!'

The Dutchman nearly fell off his chair in disbelief.

'One pound fifty? You're crazy, lake-a-picker. You guys need some psychiatric help.'

The forensics team thought they had quickly identified the body of the last man I pulled up as he had only one testicle but, shortly afterwards, when they went through all the medical files, it turned out there were two men with one testicle aboard the *Betelgeuse*.

A few days later, as we were about to get into the water, we heard a Mayday call on the radio. One of the Dutch divers had been using welding equipment to patch a hole in the hull of the *Betelgeuse* when a vacuum formed, resulting in an underwater explosion. Within seconds of the call I saw the standby diver, who had been watching his colleague on video communications, jump in and bring him to the surface, but he was already dead. We never worked near the Dutch crew because they were always cutting and welding but everything was cancelled that day and nobody was allowed in the water.

\*

Towards the end of January some of those missing crew and workers began to wash up on the shore. As we were no longer bringing up bodies, the Garda Sub-Aqua Unit was sent home. While we were back lifting the barrier in the Phoenix Park, the Dutch squad performed the deepest maritime lift in Europe at the time and hauled the front portion of the *Betelgeuse* from 120 feet under the sea, then towed it 100 miles out into the ocean and scuttled it.

We were called back down to Whiddy in March to complete another ridiculously unsafe search, this time inside the remains of the massive wreck. The Dutch divers cut a hole in the middle section of the ship so that we could go in and search the accommodation level for any bodies that might have been on board when the explosion happened. Despite the fact that we only had scuba gear and could easily be trapped inside the wreck, with just a forty-minute air supply and no way of being hauled out in an emergency, we took turns to search the interior of the ship.

On our first dive, Sergeant Paddy Morrissey and John went inside the wreck while I floated outside the hole in the side, about sixty feet below the surface, and fed in thirty feet of rope to them so that they could find their way back out.

Psychologically, knowing that you have to find your way back along thirty feet of rope before you can even attempt to surface is a bigger deal than being told you have to do a straight dive of twice the depth. If you were the first diver going into a narrow corridor you always worried about getting past the other lad to get back out. Outside, I knew that if I let the rope go they would never find their way out and if the rope severed on a piece of metal or anything went wrong, they would be trapped with no air supply apart from their cylinders and were as good as gone.

Inside, most of the dormitories had been wrecked in the explosion but there were bits of corridors and partitions left standing eerily in the darkness. Paddy and John searched some of the rooms before the claustrophobic nature of the search saw Paddy turn for the exit in panic when the rope got snagged on the corner of a partition and he thought he had been cut off.

We swapped over and I went in later on but we didn't find anyone in the wreckage. In total, forty-two French nationals, seven Irish people and one each from Britain and Holland died in Whiddy.

In my opinion the oil companies had little real interest in recovering the bodies. They just wanted to get the ship out of there and salvage it. I believe if we'd had the surface-demand gear that the navy and the Dutch guys had on Whiddy Island, we'd have found more bodies because there would never have been that fear of running out of air. If we'd had proper equipment, we could have stayed down longer, and with an umbilical air supply you could just follow your air line back to the surface. Instead, we had an air cylinder and maybe a rope tied onto us with a knot in it, if we even had enough rope.

Nowadays, leisure divers have coloured buoys floating over their heads to mark their whereabouts in the water. Back then if one of us jumped in, the lads in the dinghy were looking for bubbles to track us.

Bubbles.

In the ocean.

We were still relatively new to diving and didn't know any different. But, looking back, it was no wonder the Dutch thought we were crazy.

Salvage operations lasted for over a year, with the Dutch crew splitting the rest of the *Betelgeuse* into three parts and refloating each part with foam. It would be July 1981 before the stern was eventually brought to the surface and towed to Valencia, where it was broken up, and 1983 before the sea around Bantry was cleared of oil.

The Irish government appointed a tribunal to investigate the Whiddy Island disaster, which ultimately blamed owners Total SA for the poor condition of the *Betelgeuse* and for the explosion. According to the report, the eleven-year-old ship's hull and tanks were cracked, corroded and leaking immediately before the incident, while incorrect unloading sequences and ballasting had resulted in uneven buoyancy and the hull becoming more strained. Although lack of crew training or possible deliberate malpractice may have also been partly to blame, this was never proved as the people involved in unloading the oil had died in the explosion.

The tribunal also found that Gulf Oil's dispatcher was not at his post in the control room of the terminal and therefore could not signal the alarm when the incident happened. To hide this, false entries were made in logs, false accounts of the explosion were given and efforts were made to avoid giving statements to the gardaí.

The incident would cost the companies over $120 million in compensation claims.

Although we had the worst equipment of anyone at the Whiddy Island disaster, the garda divers, aided by the navy, were the only ones to recover bodies from the water and I was involved in three of those four recoveries. That was something to be proud of.

# The blast heard around the world

On my twenty-sixth birthday in August 1979, while on the gate in the Phoenix Park, I heard news of an armed raid on a bank close to home. One member of an IRA gang had burst into the AIB branch in Tramore while another kept watch outside and a third sat in a getaway car. Inside the bank, thirty-two-year-old Eamon Ryan, a Dublin-based civil servant who was back in Waterford visiting his mother, had cashed a cheque and was preparing to leave with his three-year-old son Peter to meet his wife Bernadette, who had gone shopping. However, at almost the same instant a hooded raider burst in. He grabbed Eamon Ryan by the throat and bundled him to the floor. Then, as the three-year-old looked on, the raider kicked the young father before standing over him and shooting him dead from twelve inches away. Outside, the second balaclava-clad IRA man used a machine gun to blow out the tyres of the local patrol car when it arrived at the scene.

Because the bank wasn't too far from where I grew up and spent my summer holidays, the robbery stuck in my head. A week or so later the bank issued a CCTV photograph of a man standing outside with a machine gun and it was circulated to every garda station to see if anybody could help identify the gang. Although the raiders were almost certainly from my neck of the woods, the picture wasn't very clear and I had no idea who the culprits were.

Three weeks later the Tramore bank robbery was all but forgotten when Lord Louis Mountbatten was murdered in Mullaghmore Harbour in County Sligo, just twelve miles from the border. The seventy-nine-year-old retired admiral was upholding his tradition of spending a month of the summer with his family at their castle, Classiebawn, in the village of Mullaghmore.

After a couple of days of bad weather the family had packed up their little green boat, the *Shadow V*, with fishing rods and picnic baskets and headed out around Mullaghmore Head for a leisurely day's fishing in the last rays of summer sun. Fifteen-year-old local boat boy Paul Maxwell was at the helm. Also on board were Mountbatten's daughter Lady Patricia Brabourne, her husband Lord John Brabourne and their fourteen-year-old twins, Nicholas and Timothy Knatchbull, as well as the twins' grandmother, the eighty-three-year-old Dowager Lady Brabourne.

Suddenly, the idyllic scene was shattered by a thunderous explosion, one that rattled the windows of houses miles away and spewed the little green boat and its seven occupants into the air, before dropping them down with a huge splash seconds later, in a mixture of splintered wooden fragments and broken bodies.

Paul Maxwell and Nicholas Knatchbull were killed instantly. Despite the best attempts of nearby fishermen who rushed to save him, the blast had almost completely blown off Lord Mountbatten's legs and he was dead before they got him back to the shore. The Dowager Lady Brabourne died from her injuries the following day.

Lord Mountbatten was Queen Elizabeth's second cousin and an uncle of Prince Philip. He was the last Viceroy of India and both a former admiral of the fleet and a former chief of the British armed forces. After the bombing, the IRA issued a statement claiming the assassination as 'one of the discriminate ways we can bring to the attention of the English people the continuing occupation of our country'.

Upon hearing the news, the Sub-Aqua Unit was immediately scrambled from Garda Headquarters and we arrived at the scene the next day. The weather was fine and the water around the bay was only about thirty feet deep, so when we did our first dive visibility was good and a bit of the bow of the *Shadow V*, the engine and some chrome portholes could be seen clearly on the seabed, but the rest of the boat was scattered all over the place.

Our first few dives were made more or less at random and spent picking up some of the larger objects from the seabed such as fishing rods, bits of picnic baskets, personal belongings and parts of the boat itself. I found a camera on one of those early dives and when the film was developed by the Technical Bureau it revealed the last few pictures of the Mountbatten family leaving the harbour.

As we widened the search area we came across a lot of kelp blocking our view of the bottom so we asked the local superintendent to buy some slash hooks for us. We would then dive with the slash hooks in the morning and cut huge sections of kelp before returning for a second dive in the afternoon, when the tide had washed it all out to sea and cleared the area for us to search unhindered. As we were laying out the anchor chain of the *Shadow V* on the bottom of the sea as a marker for these searches, I found a finger caught in one of its links.

The local hotels were booked out with the influx of international media, so the diving team was split up and stayed in various bed and breakfasts in Sligo, about twenty miles away. Paddy Morrissey and I were based in one of these B&Bs, which was run by a local garda's wife.

After dinner every night I'd have a few pints in the town, and if I was sick the next morning I'd get up early and forgo breakfast, heading off down the road on foot in an effort to walk it off before Paddy left the B&B. He'd usually catch me at the graveyard in Drumcliffe, where the poet William Butler Yeats is buried.

On one of the afternoon dives a week or so later, I found a pair of boots and brought them up. I dried them out and tried them on. The boots were only ankle high, which made them easy to walk in, and with a thick woollen lining inside them they were far more comfortable than the boots I'd been given in the garda depot, so I wore them for the next day or two.

A couple of days later one of the ballistics lads noticed the boots and asked where I'd got them, before pointing down to the insignia on the side of the boot which included the letters MBB – Mountbatten of Burma. I had been wearing Lord Mountbatten's boots. I handed them over immediately but as far as I know they were never used in evidence.

After a couple of weeks of diving every day, Sergeant Morrissey gave us a weekend off, so Susan came down for a couple of days and we booked into a hotel in Mullaghmore. I was on my best behaviour, curbing my drinking to a few pints at night.

On another Sunday off from diving I went to the garda station in Sligo to meet up with Ray Sweeney, the transport detail driver who had given me a bed the night before the *Carraig Una* inquest. Ray was driving government minister Ray MacSharry and had offered to give me a lift out to my bed and breakfast in Sligo. As we drove through Sligo town I noticed a couple standing outside a pub, both of whom I recognized as being from Waterford. I knew the woman because she lived in St John's Park, the estate next to where I grew up, and I got a flashback to the man trying to sell me an Easter Lily – a symbol of remembrance for the republican movement, associated with the Provisional IRA – in a pub in Waterford a few years earlier.

While I shrugged it off as coincidence at the time, the next morning gardaí raided a flat in Sligo and took the man – Bill Hayes – into custody. Under questioning, he admitted to acting as getaway driver in the Tramore bank robbery and was subsequently sentenced to nine years in prison.

As the investigating detective, John Courtney, knew I was from Waterford, he phoned me and asked me to go home for a week to try to find the other two bank robbers, who were believed to be Eamon Nolan and Aaron O'Connell. Unable to find any trace of the pair, I spent the rest of the week on the beer with my friends. The next week I went back up to report to John Courtney. Although I had come away empty-handed, he treated me very fairly and made sure that I wasn't out of pocket. Nolan and O'Connell were arrested and convicted a few years later and given life sentences.

We spent twenty-five days diving in Mullaghmore and by the end of it we were collecting pieces of timber from the boat no bigger than matchsticks, little flecks of green paint, wires and anything we could find in an effort to learn more about the explosion and how it had happened.

In fact the local gardaí had the person who planted the bomb on Mountbatten's boat in custody a couple of hours before the explosion even happened. Monaghan man Thomas McMahon had been stopped at a routine check-point between Granard and Longford and when he gave a false name to the guard on duty he was taken into custody on suspicion of driving a stolen car.

In Longford garda station, McMahon claimed that he didn't 'know anything about any bomb', even though the explosion was yet to happen. Having crept onto the unguarded *Shadow V* in Mullaghmore Harbour the night before, McMahon attached a radio-controlled fifty-pound bomb to Mountbatten's boat and had flecks of green paint from the boat and traces of nitroglycerine on his clothes and sand in his shoes.

The first time forensic science was used in Ireland saw McMahon convicted on evidence we had recovered from the water and given to Dr James O'Donovan from the Technical Bureau.

Although Mick Keating from ballistics had almost put

the *Shadow V* back together, he was told to burn it, as one of the superintendents had bought the prefab at St John's Road where the rebuilt boat was stored and wanted it emptied. I kept a small wooden pulley from Mountbatten's boat and when Timothy Knatchbull, the surviving twin from the explosion, came to Garda Headquarters years later, I pulled him aside and gave it to him. He later sent me a signed copy of his book about surviving the Mountbatten explosion.

Just a week or so after I returned from Mullaghmore, it seemed like most of the police force in Ireland were in the Phoenix Park, getting ready for the three-day visit of Pope John Paul II, which was commencing on 29 September. While we were away, the Popemobile had been in the garage in headquarters getting bulletproof glass installed and being armour plated. There were huge marquees all around the park in anticipation of a papal Mass being said there.

Security in the park was extremely tight in the days running up to the event. All the towers around the park were checked for snipers while helicopters hovered overhead for a couple of days prior to the visit. Hundreds of gardaí and the army were drafted in to secure the park.

The green area beside the depot hospital had a tent full of sandwiches and boilers of tea and everywhere you looked there seemed to be guards – eating sandwiches in the marquee, parading for duty in the depot or drinking in the canteen afterwards.

On the day of the Mass I was stationed in the old Technical Bureau in St John's Road. As I looked out over the wall that morning there was a steady flow of people walking towards the park from all directions. Apart from senior gardaí, of course. Although all traffic had been stopped on the outskirts of the city and people had to walk the last few miles, some officers used official passes to drive as far as St John's Road and leave their cars at the bureau.

As I was crowd spotting, I noticed two guards from headquarters in the middle of the crowd. They didn't stand out because they were dressed in uniform, though; they stood out because they were legless drunk and were trying to hold each other up at a telegraph pole before making an attempt to cross the road and collect their car, which had been parked in the bureau car park overnight. Having spent the previous night drinking in the garda canteen, the duo had made the mile or so journey from the top of the depot, down Parkgate Street, past Heuston Station and were within spitting distance of St John's Road when they got to the pole. Despite the fact that there was no traffic on the road, it took them a further ten minutes to cross to the other side. They were all set to drive home when I took the keys off the driver of their car and told them they were going nowhere.

For the rest of the morning a colleague and I kept an eye on their Volkswagen from inside a hut across the road and watched in disbelief as, first, a shoe came out the window, followed by a jacket and then a tie and a sock. After a few minutes I went over to see the two lads fast asleep in the car so I rolled down the window to give them a bit of air and left them there.

About three hours later, when a superintendent drove

in to park his car on his way to see the Pope, I sent him around the back of the building to keep him away from the lads. When I came back the Volkswagen had disappeared. I found out the next day that the pair had found a spare key in the car and had driven home through the crowds, and past numerous guards on barrier checkpoints, to Lucan.

More than one million people were estimated to have attended the first papal Mass in Ireland that day in the Phoenix Park. After it was over I strolled from St John's Road over to Steevens' Lane, stood in uniform and waved as Pope John Paul II passed on his way to a meeting with the papal nuncio.

# 12

# Getting noticed – for the
# wrong reasons

By 1980 life in the Sub-Aqua Unit had taken its toll on some of its members. When one of our best divers, my friend John Harrington, left, we were down to just six members. After the Whiddy Island disaster John had been asked to stay there for a few months in case there were more bodies recovered during the Dutch salvage operation. When the last section of the *Betelgeuse* was raised in July, John left the gardaí for good and got a job with the Dutch crew of the salvage ship the *Barracuda*.

Although the Whiddy Island and Mountbatten incidents were very good examples of why the Sub-Aqua Unit was an essential part of the police service, there were still arguments going on in the background over funding and budgets. Every time members of the Sub-Aqua Unit were called off the gate in Garda Headquarters other guards had to fill in for us on overtime rates, so garda management decided it would be cheaper if they took us off the gate and sent us to various sections of the Garda Technical Bureau instead.

When we were told of the move Donal Gibbons opted to stay on the gate and left the unit, leaving us with just five divers. New positions were advertised and Sergeant Mick Barrins was drafted in from the Garda Sub-Aqua Club, a leisure branch of the gardaí involved in sports diving, to oversee the process. Among the new recruits were Sub-Aqua Club members Aidan O'Dea and Tommy Lillis from Clare, Phil Purcell from Dublin and John Conaty from Cavan. Having come from sports diving clubs, the new recruits didn't have the skillset needed for the kind of work they would be doing in the Sub-Aqua Unit so we had to familiarize them with search-diving techniques by bringing them out to the Liffey for some training dives early on.

Our first real search that year was in January for a woman, Phyllis Murphy, who had gone missing just before Christmas. Phyllis had gone into Newbridge on Saturday, 22 December, to buy Christmas presents for her family and to visit friends. At around half past six that evening, she waited at the bus stop opposite the Keadeen Hotel for the bus home to Kildare town. It was the last time she was ever seen alive. A member of the public found her bag of Christmas presents about eight miles from the Curragh, where they had been thrown over the wall of an estate in Brannockstown.

We searched rivers, lakes, wells and ponds as well carrying out land searches on the wide-open plains of the Curragh, where her woollen mittens were found with her bus fare still tucked inside one of them.

On 17 January, almost a month after she disappeared, groups of gardaí were walking in search lines along each side of the road on the Wicklow Gap when they found Phyllis Murphy's naked body on the edge of a wood. She had been raped, strangled and dumped over thirty miles away from where she had disappeared. Blood samples were taken from over forty suspects but there was no such thing as DNA testing back then and her killer remained free. (Nearly twenty-three years later advances in DNA testing led to the conviction of a local man, John Crerar, for her murder.)

In June, one of the new diving recruits, Tommy Lillis, was due to get married down in Ennis while the rest of the unit were called out to nearby Lissycasey in County Clare on the weekend of the wedding after a young woman from Quin, Margaret Ayers, was murdered. A seventeen-year-old local hurler, Patrick Hogan, had been charged with the murder by the time we got there – he had admitted to having had a row with Margaret and throwing her body down a water-filled mineshaft. The murder squad was relying on us to find the body since, apart from the vital importance to her family of having a body to bury, it was also crucial to making the case against the killer.

When we got to where he said he had dumped the body we found a deep hole in the ground protected by a wire fence to stop people falling into it. Having been drinking the night before, I was feeling a bit seedy as I donned my dive gear. Although I wanted to go in, there were a few officers around, as well as the state pathologist, so, as the man in charge, Paddy Morrissey declined my offer and got down the shaft himself.

Paddy went down into the darkness on a rope but was back up within minutes as he had been hit by bricks falling on top of him from various ledges along the wall of the shaft as he went down. On his second dive, however, he found Margaret's body lying on a ledge about thirty feet down.

When we hauled up the body the state pathologist John Harbison wouldn't allow us to put her into the fibreglass coffin brought to the site by the local undertaker, as he wanted to keep any forensic evidence intact. So we wrapped her in polythene sheeting instead, and while she was covered and brought to the mortuary in the hearse we took the coffin, put it into the Bedford and brought it back to the West County Hotel in Ennis, where Lillo's wedding was in full swing and we had been booked in to stay during the search period.

When we arrived, we leaned the coffin up against the wall of the hotel, where I got into it and posed for a photograph with a cigar and a cap on me as the wedding went on in the background behind us.

After a few pints in the hotel bar, we went to go down the town later that night but were told by the hotel bouncers that they couldn't open the doors as there was a riot going on outside. After a couple of minutes of arguing with them, without telling them we were gardaí, we persuaded the bouncers to let us out, after which they promptly locked the doors behind us. Outside, we were confronted by a motorbike gang who had been laying boots into a young lad near the door as his sister cowered over him, trying to protect him.

The arrival of six or seven unknown men on the scene pushed them back a bit but, as we shouted at the gang to get the fuck out of there, I noticed one of them wrapping a studded belt around his knuckles. He rushed past me to kick the youngster on the ground again but I drew back my fist and caught him with a smack in the face, sending him to the ground like a sack of spuds. When a female gang member came running at me, another guard dropped her with a kick in the privates and the group began to disperse. We picked up the young lad, helped him out to the car park and put him and his sister into his car.

The two of them looked on in bewilderment as we bailed into the battered old Bedford and left the car park with blue lights flashing and sirens wailing. The gang that had been involved in the row looked just as stunned when we drove past them a few minutes later, beeping and giving them the finger out the window on our way into town.

Shortly after I got home from Clare, Susan informed me that I was going to be a father for the first time and we celebrated by going out for a meal. In theory my days of going on the lash with the lads were coming to an end. In practice nothing much changed.

A few weeks later the entire garda force was left reeling when two gardaí, Henry Byrne and John Morley, were shot dead in County Roscommon. Henry Byrne had been a couple of weeks ahead of me in Templemore and based in nearby Belturbet while I was in Ballyconnell, so his killing was particularly shocking to me.

The two men, and their colleagues Derek O'Kelly and Sergeant Mick O'Malley, were on their way from Castlerea garda station to the scene of an armed bank raid in

Ballaghaderreen, twelve miles away, when their patrol car crashed into the raiders' car at a crossroads outside Lough-glynn, about halfway to Ballaghaderreen. Immediately after the impact, as a stunned Harry Byrne opened his door to get out of the car, one of the raiders shot him dead through the opening. John Morley was carrying an Uzi and shouted at one of the three fleeing raiders to stop. Instead the man turned and opened fire, wounding him in the leg. John, a former Mayo footballer, bled to death on his way to hospital.

The three raiders continued to run across the country-side. Two of them, Paddy McCann and Colm O'Shea, were arrested close to the scene, leaving a third raider still on the run. The Sub-Aqua Unit was called in the next day to help in the search for the £35,000 stolen from the bank, the weapons used in the murders and the third raider. The gardaí also brought trainee recruits up from Templemore to help in these searches and I can remember being in a long row of about a hundred guards, walking in the direc-tion the gang member had fled, as the superintendent in charge bellowed at us to hold the line. We walked seven miles through ditches and bogs but found nothing.

Nearly two weeks later Peter Pringle, a former member of the IRA, who also had links to the INLA, was arrested in a house in Galway, with his beard shaved and his hair dyed. His clothes had been recently washed, so forensics took the filters out of the washing machine in the house and matched fibres from a jumper to those found in the car at the scene. When the case went to trial Detective Ser-geant Connolly told the court that Pringle, the son of a garda, told him: 'I know that you know that I was involved but, on the advice of my solicitor, I'm saying nothing.'

Along with the other two, Pringle was convicted of capital murder and sentenced to the death penalty – the statutory sentence for killing a member of An Garda Síochána. The sentences were later commuted to forty years' imprisonment. Pringle subsequently contested both the forensic aspects of his case and his apparent confession and his conviction was overturned by the Court of Criminal Appeal in 1995. The other two were released in 2013.

The second wave of divers slowly got a bit more experience in the water and we spent four days in the sea off Howth looking for a poker that a man used to kill his mother, as well as searches for knives and other pieces of evidence in various rivers around the country.

In November, the unit was called down to the Blue Pool, an infamous fishing spot in west Clare, to search for a father and daughter who had been washed into the sea while fishing. The Blue Pool is the name given to a spot along the cliff between Doonbeg and Kilkee where people clamber down the cliff face to a flat rock ledge twenty feet below and fish for mackerel in the Atlantic. Despite the slippery surface on the rocks and ledges, especially after a shower of rain, and the fact that numerous people had already been dragged into the ocean by freak waves over the years, locals had a saying that you could catch mackerel with a shovel down there so it didn't stop people fishing.

The McMahon family, a father, son and daughter, had been fishing on a ledge that weekend when a freak wave came in and dragged them all into the water. The son survived but the other two were swept out to sea and drowned. Myself and Jim Brennan, one of the original squad and a very strong diver from Cork, went in together on one of the dives and dropped down the hundred or so feet to the seabed and began to search the area.

As we were coming towards the end of our dive time, I got an unexpected tap on the shoulder from Jim. From the gestures he was making I knew there was something wrong and it soon became apparent that his regulator was no longer working properly and he was finding it hard to breathe.

Although regulators with a spare demand valve had been in existence since 1966, the garda diving budget didn't stretch to such luxuries, so if our single-valve mouthpiece failed underwater you either shared somebody else's or drowned. I looked at Jim and knew that the only way he was going to get to the surface alive was if we shared my air supply – a technique known as 'buddy breathing'.

Although we had trained for such an occurrence back in the ALSAA pool in Dublin airport almost six years previously, if something went wrong in the pool, you could simply stand up out of the water and breathe in; nothing like this had ever happened in a search situation before. We had all heard stories over the years of divers' equipment failing and I was aware that the donor in a buddy-breathing situation is almost always the one at risk, because once you hand over your regulator to the other diver to take a few breaths, they can be afraid to return it. Still, I put my arm round Jim and, after a few deep breaths, took out my

I'm pictured on my mother's lap in this 1955 family portrait, which also includes my older siblings Myles, Eileen and Maureen. Despite being sandwiched between those three and my younger brothers Philip and Noel, I somehow grew up to become the apple of my mother's eye.

A confirmation portrait. I'm wearing my Scoil Lorcáin uniform. By the time I'd gone into sixth class, my friends and I could scrape together the few pence required to make our way out to Tramore on the bus and spend the day on the beach and swimming in the sea.

Aged about five and looking like butter wouldn't melt in my mouth.

At the beginning of 1972, I got this photo taken to send with job applications. My mother told me that 1,000 new jobs were to be made available in An Garda Síochána. To please her, I got an extra print and applied for a job in the guards as well.

The formal picture with my parents taken on the day of my passing-out in Templemore in September 1972. This photo took pride of place in my parents' house ever after.

With my graduating class in Templemore. I'm in the front row, second in from the right. The need for extra gardaí, arising out of the Troubles, had led to a reduction in the minimum height requirement. I just about made it in and was the shortest garda in my class.

Training for the first Garda Sub-Aqua Unit at Dalkey, County Dublin in August 1974. We spent days at Bullock Harbour learning how to jump off the pier with a cylinder and mask on. I'm facing out and my colleague Donal Gibbons is on the left.

I'm second from the left in this picture taken at Bullock Harbour. We're wearing wetsuits that were totally unsuitable for open-water diving. They came in kit form and we had to stick them together ourselves! The yellow tape seals the joins.

Here I'm at the first operation of the Sub-Aqua Unit at the European Spear Fishing Championships at Kilkee.

Susan and I married in July 1978. Susan's right arm is in plaster under the chiffon sleeve of her dress. Two days before the wedding, driving while hung-over, I had crashed the car when we were returning from a visit to her family in Fermanagh. Susan ended up with a broken collarbone and broken fingers. We had to change our honeymoon plans.

Susan pictured in the driveway of our first home in Blanchardstown. Behind her is the car I wrote off two days before our wedding. I was keeping it for parts!

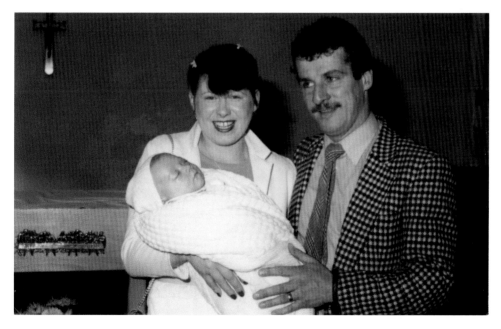

Thomas's christening in May 1981. He was the first of our two sons and was born – two months early – in January 1981. Philip's arrival, shortly after Christmas 1990, completed our family.

After a stressful dive at Whiddy Island in January 1979. The explosion of the oil tanker *Betelgeuse* was Ireland's biggest ever maritime disaster. I'm wearing a borrowed drysuit. It had no stabilizer jacket and was three sizes too big. I reverted to my wetsuit the next day.

Fellow Sub-Aqua Unit member John Harrington (*left*) and me at Whiddy. The day after our test dive we jumped in with our wetsuits covered in plastic overalls in a laughable effort to protect them from the oil. I couldn't see anything with the oil and gunk on the seabed and had to feel around in the darkness. I came upon an object that – when I lifted it – I discovered was a body. As I got nearer the surface, I realized I didn't have a full body under my arm. It was the first of just four bodies that were found and I was involved in three of those recoveries.

A bunch of garda and navy divers at Whiddy. I'm in the middle of the second row. The navy guys also had better kit than us. Our sub-standard equipment was a source of amazement to the Dutch company that was salvaging the ship for its owners. I believe if we'd had better gear we'd have found more bodies.

The 924-foot *Betelgeuse* was split in half by the explosion at Whiddy and this shows about a third of it that was still above water. The arrow is pointing at the Garda Sub-Aqua Unit's nine-foot inflatable dinghy on the deck.

In July 1980 the entire garda force was left reeling when two gardaí, Henry Byrne and John Morley, were shot dead in Loughglynn, Co Roscommon after an armed raid on a bank in Ballaghaderreen. The Sub-Aqua Unit was called in to help search for the stolen money, the weapons used in the murder and the third raider. Picture shows (*left to right*) John Conaty, me, Phil Nalty and Jim Brennan.

With best pal Declan Schutte ahead of an FAI Cup clash between the garda soccer team and Derry City in February 1986. There was a national debate about a garda team travelling across the border. When the Ulster Volunteer Force issued a death threat against the team, the government was unsure whether to permit the trip, but Deputy Commissioner Eamonn Doherty persuaded the authorities it would be fine. Although I was injured our manager rewarded my loyalty over the years by keeping me in the squad, so I travelled to the once-in-a-lifetime fixture as a substitute.

Searching for evidence in Mullaghmore Harbour after the assassination of Lord Louis Mountbatten. I'm in the water and Donal Gibbons, Jim Brennan and Sgt Paddy Morrissey are in the boat. The bomber was located on the headland overlooking the water and detonated the bomb from there.

Sub-Aqua Unit member Jim Brennan (*right*) and a local garda (*left*) as they guide in engine remains of Lord Mountbatten's boat, the *Shadow V*. The explosion also killed local boat-boy Paul Maxell, Lord Mountbatten's grandson Nicholas Knatchbull, and Nicholas Knatchbull's paternal grandmother, Lady Doreen Brabourne.

Our primitive kit in the mid-1970s: I'm wearing a half-face mask and snorkel; a decompression meter on my right wrist and depth gauge and compass on my left. And no gloves.

Diving is physically demanding so, even though I continued to drink, I tried to stay fit. I had boxed as a youngster and continued to do so through the 1970s. Here I am training for the garda championships at the garda gym in the mid-1970s.

Not exactly *Miami Vice* – on a job in the Aran Islands in the early 1980s.

Looking a bit worse for wear during a session at the European Police Cycling Championship. And this was after I had finally given up drinking!

Susan and I socializing in the late 1980s. I made a few attempts to kick the drink before I finally managed it in 1989. Susan was very patient with me.

There, but for the grace of God, go I. This picture, taken in St Peter's Square when I was in Rome for the 1990 World Cup, is a constant reminder of where I could have ended up if I had continued drinking.

Winning the annual Hamper Race in Carrick-on-Suir, where I exceeded all expectations to beat John O'Brien from Carlow (*left*) and former Tour de France green jersey winner and world number one Sean Kelly (*right*) to win the race.

Cycling became a passion. I raced in the veteran (over-40) category. I won the national veterans' championship in 1993. Here I am with some of my trophies from 1997–8, my best season.

I was a Garda Sports Star of the Year in the cycling category in 1997.

I can't blame drink for the pants! Here with the Bohermeen Waller Cup in March 2000.

Harold's Cross Bridge in Dublin. I'm in the water explaining that the car in the background is ready to be raised. In a fit of temper a woman had driven the new car into the Grand Canal after a row with her husband.

We finally got drysuits in the early 1980s. We got a bit giddy and blew them up! That's Phil Nalty behind me in the background.

At the launch of the new patrol boat, Colm na Córa, on the River Shannon in 1997. I'm with Commissioner Pat Byrne and Sub-Aqua Unit colleague John Conneelly.

October 2000. Duncannon Pier in Wexford during the search for a father who had driven himself and his two young sons into the water, where they all drowned. He had already stabbed the boys' mother to death. Searches like these were very upsetting.

Recovering evidence during a dive in Enniscorthy.

New Year 2001. Searching for the bodies of two little girls who had fallen through ice into Hollywood Lake in Monaghan while skating. I'm in the water on the left, holding one of the bodies. When I found the bodies both girls looked peaceful, something I was glad to be able to tell one of their mothers many months later at the inquest.

Philip, Susan and me with Thomas at his graduation from Waterford Institute of Technology in 2002. A week later he entered the Garda College and he is now a garda based in County Kilkenny.

One of my final jobs before retiring was the security check for the visit of George W. Bush to Dromoland Castle in County Clare for the annual EU–US summit. The picture also shows Garda Cathal Kavanagh.

Pictured with my siblings at my retirement do in 2004. Myles, Philip and me at the back, Maureen, Eileen and Noel at the front.

The first Garda Sub-Aqua Unit in 1974. *Left to right*: Jim Flood, Padraig Tunney, Louis Baldwin, John Harrington, Jim Brennan, Larry Keane, Mossie Moriarty, Neil Bracken, me, Paschal Scott (who later went into acting and played a garda in the TV sitcom *Killinaskully*), Donal Gibbons and Michael Carr.

A reunion of the unit in 2004 showing the same line-up (except Neil Bracken and I have swapped places). Back in 1974 an instructor who was not too impressed by my freewheeling attitude said I wouldn't make it in the unit because I was mad. By the time of this thirty-year reunion I was the only one of us still diving. But the instructor wasn't entirely wrong: although I was the last of the original crew to leave the unit, it was for the same reason.

regulator and gave it to him as we tried to make our way to the surface.

Once you leave the bottom of the seabed, currents can hold you at the same depth for a few seconds longer and it can be hard to tell whether you're actually heading towards the top at all. Although we were holding on to each other coming up and Jim was pretty calm and took his turn before handing the regulator back to me, I can remember looking at my depth gauge to discover it had stayed the same despite the fact that we had been pushing upwards for what seemed like a minute.

We were taking a couple of breaths at a time before holding it for a few seconds and slowly breathing out, and it felt like an eternity before we finally broke the surface and gulped in a few mouthfuls of air. But we had made it and survived to tell the tale. Although Jim wasn't a big drinker, a few pints in the pub nearby were called for to steady the nerves that night.

We didn't find the bodies on subsequent dives and they were later washed up along the coast.

Towards the end of the year, Susan and I were invited to a wedding in County Clare. I drove the 150 miles to Doon-beg with Susan in the front seat and Gussy Keating, Billy Keenan and their wives crammed into the back. After a good session at the wedding, we stopped in Roscrea on the way back the next day, where Susan and the others had dinner while I drank and watched a hurling match on the pub television.

After a few pints, I got into the car again and drove the

rest of the way to Dublin, dropping the others off on the way home. Once we got near the Phoenix Park and within touching distance of home, however, nothing would do me but to go in for my usual Sunday-night drinks in the garda canteen.

Susan was now five months pregnant and she was suffering terribly from back pain. Of course, I was oblivious to this and when she said she wasn't coming into the canteen, I just left her in the car in the freezing cold.

I don't remember it now, but Susan has since told me that any time another garda went past the car, she would roll down the window and tell them to send me out, but her pride wouldn't let her go in and get me herself. As she shivered outside in the car, I stayed an hour or so in the canteen with the lads, something I'm not proud of now.

Even when Susan was heavily pregnant I never refused to go on a job when I was called, and in early January 1981 I went for four days to Clonmany in Donegal looking for two men who had disappeared off a boat into the sea. As I prepared to wrap up my last dive in Donegal on the Friday night, Susan's sisters called up to light the fire for her and offered to stay in the house. Despite the worsening pain in her back, Susan insisted she was fine and the two girls left.

I came home from Donegal the next day and upon my arrival Susan got dressed up and we went to the Granite pub in Palmerstown, where we met the garda soccer team manager Vinny Hyland and his wife Imelda for our usual Saturday-night drinks. As we drank and chatted, I was still oblivious to the fact that Susan could hardly sit on the chair with the pain in her back, even when Imelda warned me to keep an eye on her.

The next morning I was up and ready for the usual Sunday-morning routine that would see Vinny and me go to watch a Leinster Senior League or AUL game in Chapelizod before going to the pub for a few pints afterwards. I was heading out the door to meet Vinny when Susan called me from the top of the stairs to tell me that her waters were breaking. She might as well have been telling me in Chinese because I hadn't a clue what she meant. I soon realized it wasn't a good sign, though, with two months left in her pregnancy.

We grabbed a bag and I helped her into the car and drove through the Phoenix Park towards Holles Street Maternity Hospital. I was going so fast that one of the traffic wardens in the park tried to jump out in front of me to slow me down. I pulled up outside the hospital, brought Susan in and was ushered into another room where six fellas were pacing up and down smoking cigarettes as if they were going out of fashion.

Susan was in a waiting room with about twenty other women and she kept going in to tell the nurse that her baby was coming but they kept sending her out. On the third or fourth time, though, they took her in, and within minutes of me sitting down with the other expectant fathers the door opened and a nurse walked over to me.

'Congratulations, Mr Lavery, you have a lovely baby boy.'

I walked in to see Susan on a makeshift bed in a small room. A nurse stood beside her with our tiny little newborn son, Thomas, in her arms. He was born two months premature and weighed a mere three pounds, so the nurse didn't give me much time to look at him before she whisked him away and took him to an incubator.

I should have been concerned about Susan, and that Thomas was premature and so small and fragile, but as soon as Susan was moved into a ward, my priority was getting to the Granite to tell Vinny that I was a father. I celebrated with Vinny and Imelda for a few hours before visiting Susan and Thomas and going back to the pub on the way home.

The next day I was starting a six-week course with the Criminal Investigation Department (CID). I woke up with a pounding headache and a queasy stomach. I felt so bad during the morning's lecture that, in the hope that it would ease my hangover, I went down to Parkgate Street and had a few pints at lunchtime before returning to the classroom for the afternoon lecture, which was given by John Courtney of the murder squad.

Having been involved in various cases with me, he had great time for me and said nothing when I nodded off at the back of the class. When the room emptied for a mid-afternoon tea break and I stayed asleep, however, he came down and gave me a shake.

'Well, Tosh? I hear the wife had a baby. Do you want to go home?' he asked.

'Nah, I'm all right,' I mumbled.

But John wasn't the only one who had noticed my behaviour that day and I was called into the chief superintendent's office shortly after.

'Your wife just had a baby,' said the chief super, 'so if

you want to put this course off you can do it again later on in the year.'

Again, I reassured him that I would be fine and wanted to continue on the course, but as I was leaving the office foyer Eamonn Moriarty, a clerical officer I knew, pulled me aside.

'They're on your house, Tosh. They were talking about your drinking, so the best thing you can do is get stuck into that course and show them.'

From day one, I had always been a binge drinker and could stop if I had something to achieve, so I never really thought I had a problem with alcohol and simply decided I would stop drinking there and then. For the next five weeks I didn't touch a drop of alcohol and spent my spare time visiting our new addition, Thomas, in hospital with Susan and also put in a good bit of studying for the end-of-course exams.

During that CID course, a member of the garda drugs squad, which was only a five- or six-man crew based in Dublin Castle, came in with a tray of drugs and handed them around the class for us to look at and familiarize ourselves with.

'Every one of you, through members of your own family, will come across drugs within ten years,' he announced.

When I told him of my experience with the New York cops a couple of years previously and how they had told me the same thing, he seemed impressed that somebody backed up his theory, but the rest of the class just sniggered behind my back for speaking up.

Having stayed sober throughout, five weeks later, I

finished fourth in the class (a class that included a future garda commissioner, Fachtna Murphy) and celebrated by getting drunk at the post-course get-together in the Garda Club.

# 13

## 'The madness factor'

When we finally got to bring Thomas home in February 1981 it was snowing, and as our house had been built in the late seventies there was little or no insulation in it, so the only way to keep our tiny baby warm was to light the fire and stay in the sitting room. Like most first-time parents, the reality of being responsible for this little man's welfare was a bit of a shock to the system for both of us. Susan, though, was brilliant. She was a natural mother and she never batted an eyelid about anything, even when I went off on jobs, leaving her literally holding the baby.

Of course it still never occurred to me to put my family before the job. When I look back now, one of my failings while in the Sub-Aqua Unit was that I was such a loyal foot soldier. When the phone rang and I was asked to go and search for somebody, I never hesitated, no matter what was coming up, be it a wedding, anniversary, birthday or even Christmas. Even now that I had a little family of my own to look after, I couldn't understand other lads in the unit wanting to go home from a search to be with their families.

The nature of the job meant that we could be down the country for long periods, with just the odd day trip home

or a visit from your wife on one of those weekends. But it
didn't bother me. I wanted to get the job done, find the
missing person, before I ever thought about going home.
If I was told that we were going to be called off a search
before we found somebody, I would often tip off the missing person's relatives and tell them to go to their local TD
and complain. The next morning we would be told that we
were given a reprieve and would be staying in the area for
a few more days. For me, that meant a few more days
searching and, more often than not, a few more nights in
the pub. It wasn't until later in life that I appreciated what
a good job Susan had done at home on her own while I
was away.

Although the unit had been regenerated with new
blood, we hadn't got any better equipment, were still diving in inferior wetsuits and waiting on the promised Van
Hool bus and better boats. On a dive at Lacken pier in Killala, County Mayo, though, a chance incident looked as if
it might change all that. While searching for two men who
had fallen into the sea, Phil Purcell and I were getting
changed in the back of the old Bedford van when former
garda detective and Fianna Fáil TD Seán Doherty, or 'the
Doc', as he was known, arrived at the dive site with his
wife. Coming to thank us for our help in the search, the
Doc pulled open the back door of the van to reveal two
naked divers to his mortified spouse.

After getting changed, I got out of the van and apologized to the woman but she was more interested in our
own welfare: 'Oh my God, these men are working in atrocious conditions, Seán. You'll have to do something about

this. Getting changed in the back of a van after diving in the sea. Something will have to be done. Those poor men!'

After searching for four days and losing two cylinders to a rough sea, we spent our final night in Killala being bought drinks in Fianna Fáil councillor Seán Golden's pub, where I can remember having so many hot whiskeys in front of me that half of them had gone cold.

As is the way with most politicians, the Doc, then a junior minister in the Department of Justice, promised us the sun, moon and stars. When he took on the justice portfolio as minister the following year, I thought we were finally going to get properly kitted out. However, the only thing we ever got off him was a hangover in Killala.

As during the CID course earlier in the year, there were periods when I gave up drinking for various lengths of time, usually when I had something coming up that I could target. One such event was the 1981 Dublin City Marathon, the second ever running of the event. Some of the guards around headquarters had run the inaugural marathon the year before and were signed up to do it again. A couple of the lads in the diving unit were also contemplating taking part and, thinking of it as a great way to stay fit, I entered with them.

When my brother Philip heard I was going to run the marathon, he decided that he would join me in Dublin on the day, so, with eight weeks to go to the race, he started training on his own in Waterford while I began pounding the roads around the Phoenix Park whenever I got the chance. I began with six- or seven-mile runs through the park at lunchtime, sometimes pacing myself behind one of the lads in the garda Gaelic football team, Hughie White.

When we were called down the country on a job, a few of us would go for a run in the evenings afterwards. None of us had high-visibility jackets or vests and we stopped running for ten days after Phil Nalty, Aidan O'Dea and I were nearly wiped out by a car in the dark country roads of Mayo one evening.

After the incident, we were having a couple of pints one night and reasoned that, as we were diving during the day, it would be enough exercise to see us through the twenty-six-mile run later in the month and training was put off for about a week.

As I always looked upon exercise or physical training as part of my job, I never thought much about running round the park while on duty on the gate, although the job didn't look on it that way.

While on the gate one night leading up to the marathon, I decided to go for a run at four in the morning. When I arrived back to an irate sergeant, who gave out to me for leaving the premises, I told him that I was on my break and was entitled to do my run. His argument was that I wasn't allowed outside the depot while on duty, while I told him I was keeping fit for my job. I figured if I hadn't been out running I would just have been wandering around the depot and more than likely would have ended up in the canteen anyway.

I stopped drinking with seventeen days to go and gradually built up my runs around the park so that I completed a seventeen-miler while on duty one Saturday shortly before the event.

On the day of the race, I met quite a few gardaí from various sections of the force as I lined up with my brother in Stephen's Green. At the time, the Garda rowing team had a strong crew of runners – including Paul Myles and legendary Olympian and international rower Frank Moore, who had carried the tricolour at the 1976 Olympics – who trained at the Garda Boat Club every Sunday morning, often racing each other the twenty-three miles to New-castle and back.

As we ran past the Mullingar House in Chapelizod in the opening miles, an off-duty garda, Mick Dunne, stood at the door waving a pint of lager in the air as we went by.

'Hey, Lavery, here's a pint of lager for ya!'

We then turned into the Phoenix Park and as it was a bank holiday Monday most of the lads from around the depot came out to cheer us on and take photos. As we ran through the park towards Cabra, Philly was wrecked and began moaning to me about not having the training miles done, but I was too busy waving and shouting at everyone I knew going along the road to pay any attention.

We had a plan to run the first half at a steady pace and I told him to stick to the plan. We caught and passed Aidan in Ballymun and we even passed one of the boat club training group a few miles later.

Although we ran the second half of the marathon eleven minutes faster than the first, by the time we got to Fairview, with about six miles to go, we were struggling into what felt like a gale-force headwind. As we dragged ourselves over a little bridge that you wouldn't even notice was there on an ordinary day, I thought I'd never get to the line.

Eddie Finucane, an older guard from the swimming club, came up alongside us. If I was under a bit of pressure before, Eddie made it twice as bad. All dressed in black and about thirteen years older than me, Eddie seemed to be running easier than us but immediately started complaining about pains in his knees and his back and after a few minutes almost had us convinced that we had them too.

'You go ahead, Eddie,' I said. 'You're flying.'

Eddie ran off up the road, but two minutes later we passed him sprawled on the ground up against a bus with an on-duty guard leaning over him to see if he was all right. Philly and I trickled past him and aimed ourselves towards the finish but in Amiens Street Philly, who had been struggling for the first hour and a half, suddenly upped the pace. He then left me behind as we headed towards the line in Stephen's Green, finishing a minute and a half ahead of me to record a time of three hours and forty-one and a half minutes.

Neil Cusack won the race in two hours, thirteen minutes and fifty-nine seconds, while Paul Myles set a new garda record of two and a half hours that stood for years afterwards. As I crossed the line, Frank Moore, the former Olympian, sat in an oxygen tent just past the finish and another garda from the Garda Boat Club running group lay exhausted nearby. I collected my finisher's medal, threw a tinfoil blanket around myself and walked into

Hourican's Bar on Leeson Street, where I ordered a pint of Heineken.

Having been in the Phoenix Park earlier with Thomas, who was now ten months old, Susan was at the finish and she and some of the lads from the depot joined us inside afterwards. Aidan O'Dea had been doing six-minute miles but struggled over the last five and was finding it hard to sip a cup of tea as I skulled my first two pints of lager. After drinking another four, I put on a tracksuit and Susan and I got into the car and headed for home.

As we passed the Phoenix Park a few minutes later we stopped at the Hole in the Wall pub and I had another two pints there before finally going home and falling asleep for a couple of hours. Then, refreshed after my nap, I got up, got back into the car and spent the rest of the night in the garda canteen.

Philly headed back to Waterford the next morning while I was due to start work at nine. Feeling a bit seedy from the night before, I went to the canteen in the bureau for a cup of tea to wake me up. I couldn't get over how many lads around the depot were suffering from the previous day's run. Some were limping, some were hobbling and some were just sitting, unable to put weight on their legs at all. Apart from being hung-over, there wasn't much wrong with me and I spent the morning wondering what the hell was up with them.

The icing on the cake for me was seeing my photo on the front cover of the *Garda Review* running alongside Aidan and Philly a few weeks later.

*

Shortly after finishing the marathon we were called out to Enniscorthy in County Wexford to search for a knife used in a murder. Two men had been drinking in a pub all day when a fight broke out between them. One had stabbed the other and thrown the murder weapon into the river Slaney.

As I was the youngest and therefore felt I had the best chance of finding the knife, I wanted to get into the water to carry out the search and there was a bit of an argument between myself and Sergeant Morrissey over who would go in.

Eventually, we laid out a rope in the river, which was pretty shallow, and I began a painstakingly slow search, going over and back, looking for the knife. On the far side of the river was a piggery and as I searched I could hear the squeal of the pigs as they got slaughtered and every few minutes the river would turn red as blood and shit ran into it.

After I'd used up a cylinder of air, Paddy, who was as stubborn as I was, insisted on getting in but I wouldn't come out and instead grabbed another cylinder and spent another hour looking for the knife before surfacing triumphantly with the weapon.

Having been on the CID course at the start of the year, I remembered being told to keep the weapon in the water it was found in and to put it into a sealed tin. A piece of fibre from the assailant's jumper was later found on the knife and he was duly convicted.

The year ended with a five-day trip back to Donegal, when a third trawler, the *Skifford*, sank near Burtonport with nine crew members on board. When it became apparent that the *Skifjord* had run aground at around 3 a.m., the crew of the nearby *Arkansas* and the *Autumn Glory* came to their aid, but, even though they reached the marooned trawler within ten minutes, the reef between the boats meant they couldn't throw a safety line across to them. With the crew of the *Skifjord* hanging on to the rails, the sea came up onto the deck and washed them off the boat.

Chef Standish O'Grady managed to tie two buoys together from the fishing nets and he and Gerry Laverty made it to the island of Inishinny, where they broke into a cottage and were later found by a search party. John McGuinness and Eamonn Mullin also swam towards the mainland and, despite swallowing diesel from the downed trawler, they stayed afloat and were pulled from the water by Sergeant Donal Ward and some of the locals, including the father of a young Packie Bonner, the Republic of Ireland goalkeeper.

Tony O'Brien had been swimming with McGuinness and Mullin but is thought to have struck a submerged rock and was knocked unconscious. His body was recovered at approximately 7.30 a.m. while the body of Jimmy Laverty was found about two and a half hours later.

When I heard the news on the radio in the Garda Headquarters, my mind flashed back to the *Evelyn Marie* and *Carraig Una* disasters. It was heartbreaking to think that this small tight-knit fishing community had been hit by a third devastating tragedy.

When we arrived from Dublin, there was another argument on the shore as Sergeant Morrissey refused to let

Aidan O'Dea and Phil Purcell dive as he said they hadn't enough experience. I asked him how they were going to get any experience if he didn't let them dive, but when Purcell argued with him in the pub that night, Morrissey told him to go home before eventually giving in and letting him stay the next morning.

I was the first one into the water, followed shortly by Sergeant Morrissey, but we returned to the surface minutes later as he thought the boat was listing in the waves and was afraid it might capsize on top of us. After a bit of discussion, we dived again and I was first onto the deck of the sunken trawler, which was lying on its starboard side, having slid down what the locals called the 'Mad Reef' – a reef between Arranmore and Burtonport – to its final resting place on the seabed.

While I had gone to the bow of the ship, Patrick Kyles, a civilian diver from Burtonport, went to the stern and within minutes was heading for the surface with a body. There was a small aluminium lifeboat sitting in the sand next to the ship with a lovely new rope coiled up on the deck and, with budgetary constraints still in mind, I earmarked it for use in future searches. It might seem odd to be thinking like that in the middle of a search for bodies, but after so long on the job it was second nature to me to wonder how we could be more effective.

That night we met some of the lads from the area who had been involved with the *Evelyn Marie* and *Carraig Una* searches and they brought us out to Paddy Neely's pub in the middle of the mountains. An old-time pub with a big open fire, Neely's never closed and, with no car to go home in, it was the only time I ever saw my colleague Jim Brennan drunk. Just as things began to quieten down in the early hours of the morning, the young people from the area arrived in on their way home from a disco and the pub was packed again. Although we stayed up there and dived for a few more days, gales and heavy seas hampered searches and no more bodies were found.

The New Year brought with it one of the biggest snow-storms to hit the east coast of Ireland and January 1982 saw temperatures reach a record minus twenty degrees at the weather station in the Phoenix Park. As blocks of ice floated down the Liffey, and huge snowdrifts piled over eight feet high in places along the roadside, the country was brought to a standstill for almost a fortnight.

Even with the mobilization of 500 soldiers (nicknamed 'storm troopers' by the national media) and six snow-mobiles (donated by the Canadian government), many people were left isolated in their homes, with their home heating supply frozen, while hundreds of cars were aban-doned around the country. I had never seen a snowdrift in my life before, but soon we had six feet of snow climbing over the wall in our back garden in Blanchardstown.

In the midst of this storm, the diving unit was called out to Wexford, where two brothers and their three teen-age sons had been out duck shooting on Tacumshane Lake, near Kilmore Quay, when their boat overturned in the icy water and they had all drowned.

With twenty-foot-high drifts of snow lining the roads, we had to get a 4x4 jeep from the garda garage, while the navy was also called out from Cork, in case we were unable to get there. After making our way down to Wexford, the last few miles towards Kilmore Quay and the lake were on back roads and the conditions were so treacherous that we were travelling at a snail's pace.

When we arrived at the lakeshore, there were a couple of horse boxes set up in the car park with hot food being prepared for the people who were already out searching along the shoreline. As the lake had frozen solid overnight, a steel boat with an engine on it had to be brought over from Kilmore Quay to break through the ice before we could begin our search. As things were getting organized a local woman, Mrs Parle, gave us a cup of coffee; when I took a sip I realized she had laced it with brandy in an effort to warm us up.

Up until then, none of the new divers had seen a dead body so there was a bit of trepidation on the shoreline as they began to realize that there were five of them out there somewhere in the water. As the missing party's boat had been found floating upside down in the water, there was no way of knowing where it had overturned, so we began the search by being towed across the bottom of the huge lake on a bar tied onto the back of the steel boat in the hope that we would see something to tell us where the boat had capsized. I was paired up with two civilian divers for my first search and, as the two lads stepped gingerly into the icy cold water in their brand-new sealed drysuits with layers of warm clothing underneath, I stepped out in my flimsy wetsuit.

Although the theory behind the wetsuit was that it

would allow in a layer of water that would rise to body temperature and keep you reasonably warm, it never really worked and it certainly wasn't going to work in such low temperatures, particularly in a situation where we were being towed and weren't using our arms or legs. As I was already frozen before I got into the lake, the constant flow of icy water through the suit almost gave me hypothermia but what I now call 'the madness factor' took over. Not wanting to let the civvies alongside me see how cold I really was, and determined to last longer on the bar than them, I survived the next few days by drinking copious amounts of Mrs Parle's coffee and as many hot whiskeys as were offered to me by the local fishermen.

After diving each day, everyone would adjourn to the local pub before driving back to Wexford town and our accommodation in White's Hotel. The next morning's hangover was cured with another couple of early-morning coffees from Mrs Parle. Finally, a few mornings in, while I was being dragged through the icy water, I saw the engine of the boat underneath me and let go of the bar. As the water was shallow enough where I'd found it, I stood up and raised the engine up over my head to show everyone where the boat had overturned.

Within a couple of hours all five bodies were recovered and placed in a big freezer unit we had positioned at the side of the lake, to be collected by the undertaker. Meanwhile the garda and navy divers spent the afternoon in the pub before going to the chapel for the removals that evening.

# 14

# Feeding the fish

A broken collarbone suffered while playing in the Leinster Senior League with the garda soccer team kept me out of the water for a few weeks in the summer of 1982. Off work with the injury one day, I was sitting at home in Blanchardstown when my brother Noel rang me to say that one of my best pals in Waterford, Nicky Power, had gone out onto the river Suir the night before and drowned.

I got into my car and headed to Waterford, where I met up with John Hennessy. He told me how he and Nicky had obtained a currach with an engine on it in Wexford a few days before so that they could poach for fish on the river at night. They had previously been using a net from the shore and had also been relieving another well-known poacher, who had a big net on a part of the river known as Peg's Hole, of most of his catch any time he was away.

To have the newly acquired boat was a big bonus and Henno and Nicky hid it down by the Goldcrust bakery on the banks of the river. A couple of nights after stashing the boat they were having a few drinks and planning their first poaching spree when Nicky's brother Pudgey arrived on the scene. After Henno had gone home, Pudgey and Nicky decided to go down and get the boat to search the big net at Peg's Hole, although Henno, before he left, had already warned Nicky that he was in no fit state to go near the river. Later that night, the boat ended up on the rocks at the side of the river and, while Pudgey scrambled to safety, Nicky ended up in the water and drowned.

Although I couldn't get into the water with my broken collarbone, the next morning I joined John and a few locals on a little twelve-foot boat owned and skippered by a friend of ours, Danny Reynolds, and we went up and down the river searching for Nicky. We found the boat with the rear portion busted off it and the engine gone, which gave credence to a theory John had, that the boat had been rammed by another poacher on the river.

After a night of drinking with John, I returned to the river the next morning and, in anger at Nicky's death, and at not being able to get into the water to look for him, I took a hatchet to the remains of the boat, which the local guards had said they were finished with, and I sank it.

We searched for a fortnight but didn't find Nicky, and his body eventually surfaced near Peg's Hole weeks later. Although John was an undertaker, when Nicky was found he wouldn't go down to identify the body and asked me to do it instead. I went to Ardkeen Hospital with young Michael Hennessy, John's nephew. When the body was produced I had a flashback to him telling me in a pub one night, shortly after I got into the Garda Sub-Aqua Unit, that I'd never be searching for him in any river.

By the time I got back to diving a few weeks later, the Sub-Aqua Unit had finally got new drysuits, a luxury to us after eight years of hardship. Having a sealed drysuit meant that we could also wear a 'woolly bear', like a thermal onesie, underneath to keep us warm in extreme temperatures.

Throughout the year the unit continued to evolve. Mick Barrins took over as sergeant when Paddy Morrissey left the unit for a posting in Collon in County Louth and, with Jim Brennan leaving the guards altogether and Padraig Tunney moving to Canada, John 'Jasper' Conneelly and Frankie Quinn were added to the roster.

In the space of two years I had gone from being one of the two youngest in the unit to being the oldest and most experienced garda diver. I could only laugh when one of the younger lads complained one day that his drysuit was leaking after a trickle of water had run down his neck during a search.

Although Sergeant Morrissey hadn't felt some of the lads had enough experience to get into the water at the *Skifjord* disaster a few months earlier, they soon learned the hard way and in 1983 alone we pulled seventeen bodies out of the sea, rivers and lakes of Ireland.

The little town of Lisdoonvarna in County Clare accounted for almost half of that total. The Lisdoonvarna Festival was a three-day music event that ran from the late seventies and was immortalized in Christy Moore's eponymous song. The festival was in its sixth year when tragedy struck. After watching Van Morrison and Rory Gallagher perform on Sunday, 31 July, hundreds of revellers decided to walk across the fields and head to the beach at Doolin for a cooling dip in the sea. As crowds gathered around the rocks, and dozens waded out into the water on a beautiful but treacherous part of the beach known as Trá Leathain, the combination of a strong coastal current and the changing tide dragged about thirty people out of their depth and into the ocean.

Three brothers from Carlow, James, John and Eddie Dolan, who were just twenty-five, twenty-two and nineteen years old, were among eight people who drowned within minutes of having their feet swept from under them and being pulled down by the current. After lending his shorts to one of the others so that he could go swimming, a fourth brother was left on the shore. (Tragically, years after the three Dolan brothers were pulled out of the ocean in Doolin, their sister's boyfriend also drowned when he fell off a bridge in Wexford. We found his body too.)

A local fisherman, Gerry Flaherty, plucked two men from the sea that day, one alive and the other dead, while we were called out to try to recover the bodies of another seven missing. While the lads made their way down from Dublin in the van, I drove across from Waterford as I had been down visiting my mother that weekend. When I got there, the navy divers had arrived too and some of the garda lads were already kitted out, so I stayed on the surface in the boat as they searched underwater.

As bad as diving to look for dead bodies was, waiting in the boat to haul them in was worse. Visibility was good that day and between the two dive crews we found all the missing people and pretty soon they were throwing them up to me in the little dinghy as if they were mackerel. Even if I was pleased for the families involved that the bodies had been recovered, it was a traumatic experience to be standing in the boat with five bodies piled beside me.

In those days, there was no such thing as post-traumatic stress disorder (PTSD). The only thing we had to help us cope was the pub, and in Doolin afterwards we were all feted as heroes for finding the bodies and treated to free drink for the rest of the night.

Although drinking was a big part of my life, I began to realize that it wasn't something to be proud of and tried to hide it as best I could; only those close to me knew how bad it had become. If I felt myself getting inebriated in the garda canteen, I'd get into the car and go off to Cumiskeys just outside the depot gate and maybe have two drinks there. Before the barman could see how drunk I was there, I'd move to the Hole in the Wall just a few yards further down Blackhorse Avenue and after that on to a pub in Clonsilla, all the while edging my way closer to home.

I always felt physically sick after drink, but even if I was on duty I could always sneak into a toilet somewhere on the road or in headquarters and throw up. The first time I can remember vomiting underwater was during a search of the river Suir in 1983 to look for a local girl who had gone missing. I had been drinking until four in the morning after the first search with the girl's brother and a couple of other locals I knew.

Because you have to dive on the tide in the Suir, I was back in the water four hours later with one of the worst hangovers ever. Reeling and retching from the night's drinking, I managed to hold myself together until I got into the water and down to the bottom of the river bed. Here, in the dark dank water I breathed in, removed my mouthpiece and, as I breathed out, I spewed up my guts before slotting my mouthpiece back in and continuing the search. When I felt the urge again, I simply repeated the procedure. The sergeant on the bank and the rest of the unit were none the wiser.

After forty minutes of searching, though, I still felt sick, so I came up and told the sergeant that I had to go to my mother's house on a message. Instead, I went over to the early house on the docks and ordered a brandy and port and a bottle of stout to 'settle' my stomach.

After a while, I had vomiting underwater down to a fine art and, like blowing out air, I could do it anywhere. Even in a group of divers, I could do it without anyone else noticing. I would drift back off a search line to vomit and got so good at it that I would even allow for the current to take the contents of my stomach away with it so the others wouldn't see the puke floating past them.

In three or four years of getting sick underwater, I was only seen 'feeding the fish' once. A fellow diver told me years later that he nearly choked with laughter as he saw the fish following me after I'd taken out my mouthpiece and released a stream of puke in the water across the other side of the search rope.

Shortly after, I went to a cousin's funeral in Limerick and spent four days drinking and driving around the local pubs with a cousin in the front seat and another fella in the back playing a tin whistle. Eventually, after causing a bit of mayhem, the priest had to ask me to go home.

We were always kept busy with searches for murder weapons and other pieces of evidence. I was back in Ballyconnell twice at the end of the year to pull bodies out of the Woodford River in Belturbet and in Ballyconnell itself.

The start of the hunting season invariably saw us called out to a tragedy somewhere around the country and in January 1984 we were searching for four duck shooters who had disappeared on Lough Gill in County Sligo. Although I had an ear infection, I insisted on getting into the water but I was forced to get out as the pressure built up and I couldn't take the pain any more. Two of the men were found during the search while another body surfaced, badly decomposed, two years later.

That summer we were called out to Lough Mask in County Mayo, where a family had been out on the lake in an aluminium boat with no life jackets on them when it had overturned. Lough Mask is ten miles long by four miles wide and can vary in depth from about ten feet to thirty feet. While lakes like Lough Mask can look calm and serene in photographs, most of them are situated in between hills or mountains, which means that when the wind starts to blow, it funnels through the water and can create huge waves, turning the lake into a miniature ocean.

When the Flannery family's lightweight aluminium boat capsized in a deep section of the lake, they tried to cling on to the upturned hull but in the scramble for safety fifty-year-old John Flannery, his twenty-one-year-old son Oisín and ten-year-old daughter Tara drowned. With the three dead bodies lying across the upturned boat and the bodyweight of six people making it immobile, a fifteen-year-old Dubliner who had gone out with them made the tough but correct decision to push the dead bodies off the boat in the middle of the night to give those who remained alive a chance of drifting to the shore and survival. When they did this, the boat lifted and the wind blew them to the tiny island of Inishowel nearby, where they were found the next morning.

The survivors told us what had happened, so we began our search by towing around the island on a bar and, as visibility was good, we found the three bodies together in about twenty-five feet of water on the first dive. In thirty years of diving I've seen a lot of things that have faded in time, but the expression on John Flannery's face remains with me to this day. I remember him having a look of disgust on his face, as if he blamed himself for bringing his family out on the lake.

Back in the bureau, I came out of Cumiskeys one night with another guard and as we were walking through the park we found a nurse's uniform scattered in the grass. As a nurse, Bridie Gargan, had been attacked and murdered while sunbathing in the park in the summer of 1982, we decided to look around the area.

When we couldn't find anything else we went home with the plan of calling into the hospital the next morning to check it out. The next day, before I had the chance to do that, Susan found the uniform in the back of my car and thought I'd been with somebody else the night before. No matter what I said she wouldn't believe me. However, the truth was that in those years when I was drinking heavily I had zero interest in women in pubs or nightclubs: I was the stereotypical Irishman of the time, someone who would walk across ten women to get to a pint.

The next day I went to St Mary's Hospital in the park and handed the uniform in but nobody ever contacted me about it afterwards and it was soon forgotten.

In April of 1985 we got a call from the Bridewell garda station in Cork after a local man walked into the lobby, sat his baby up on the counter and told the garda on duty that he was going to do away with himself. Before the garda had time to answer, the man turned on his heels, ran out of the station and jumped into the river Lee outside. Arriving on the day after the incident, we parked near the Bridewell and got into the river at a narrow section under a nearby bridge. Diving within touching distance of each other, we came across the body within five minutes and brought him up on the bank.

Since it was a Saturday and we were on overtime, we were in no rush to go home so after we got changed we went into the station and sat down for a while. As we were having a bit of lunch and watching a football match on the television a couple of hours later, the inspector opened the door and called me out.

'That's the wrong body, Tosh!' he said.

'What do you mean, the wrong body?'

'That's not the man you were looking for. That's another fella altogether, a Mr Daly. He's not reported missing and we didn't even know he was in the water.'

We stayed for a few more days and continued searching for our initial victim, a Mr Moran. The Lee widened as we swam down along it and at the time most of Cork's sewage was being pumped into it. The further down we went, the denser the haze in the water got, until we were finally searching in a sludge of raw sewage, tampons and condoms. We didn't find Mr Moran; his body surfaced a couple of days later further down the river.

On our way to Lough Gill in Sligo to search for a gun a couple of months later, we were in the car when news came over the radio that our former sergeant Paddy Morrissey had been shot dead after a bank raid in Collon. Paddy had been on his way from Ardee courthouse after a sitting of the local court when word reached him that a robbery had taken place at the employment exchange in the town.

Michael McHugh from Crossmaglen and Noel Callan from Monaghan had carried out the raid and made off with £25,000 in a car belonging to the manager before changing to a motorbike to give them a better chance of escaping on the narrow country roads of County Louth. When Paddy saw a patrol car rushing to the scene he flagged it down and was in the back seat as they chased the raiders towards Tallanstown, where the pair fled on foot after crashing their motorbike.

While the two local cops stayed where the motorbike had crashed and a gun had been dropped on the ground, Paddy, as always, wasn't one for standing idly by and, even though he was unarmed, he took after them on foot. One of the raiders turned and shot him in the groin. Then, not content with wounding him, the gunman walked up to Paddy and shot him in the face. Paddy was forty-nine and a father of four.

Although I had plenty of arguments with Paddy over the years, they were mostly just battles of ego, but nobody could ever say he didn't do his job. Paddy was one of the very few sergeants who came into the diving unit and wasn't afraid to get into the water. In fact, most of the time our arguments were over who should get into the water first and we were probably both as stubborn as each other.

His death came as a massive shock to all of us. His funeral in Drogheda was enormous. Flowers covered the whole area surrounding his grave in Belturbet afterwards, and as a mark of respect I laid a little flag, used to mark a 'diver down', on top of his grave.

Paddy's killers, Callan and McHugh, were brought to the Special Criminal Court in December of the same year and were sentenced to death for capital murder of a garda, but, like the others before them, their sentences were later reduced to forty years in jail without remission.

A few weeks later we were back up north, this time in Buncrana in County Donegal to search for a social worker named Cyd Coulter. Cyd was a sister of the songwriter Phil Coulter. She had been celebrating her son Stephen's tenth birthday at home when a client phoned, saying that he needed her help. She never came home and for a couple of days nobody knew where she had gone until a local man saw marks on the pier where a car had hit it and it became apparent that she had been the victim of a murder-suicide by her client.

On a wet and miserable night, we dived and found the car just below the pier as a few members of the local media looked on. While Cyd Coulter's body was still inside, the male occupant was found washed up on a nearby beach.

On All-Ireland Football Final day, 22 September, I was drinking in Cumiskeys with sergeants John Creigh and Jim O'Donnell, both former inter-county hurlers. Having watched Dublin beat Kerry, we arranged to meet for a drink at lunchtime the following day. As the evening wore on, though, we all got a bit the worse for wear. As I was playing for the garda soccer team at the time, there was a bit of slagging going on over whether GAA players were fitter than soccer players.

The barman, Fintan Delaney, played Gaelic football with a local club and when I told them all I had won the 100m and 200m in the Garda Sports Day a few years back, one of the lads bet me ten pounds that Fintan would hammer me in a sprint. Rising to the bait, I soon found myself out in the back yard, where we decided that the winner would be the first one to touch a wall down the end of the alley that ran alongside the pub.

To give myself 'a better chance' of beating Fintan, who was younger than me, I decided to take my trousers off before going to the start line, where the race began with a shout from one of the lads. With ten pounds on the line, I was running as fast as I could but was so drunk I was seeing stars. When it came to touch the wall at the 'finish line', I was going too hard to stop and slammed my wrist off the wall on impact and broke it for the second time in my career.

Probably in an effort to wind me up even more, the lads gave Fintan the tenner afterwards because they said he won. Still, we drank it between us.

After the race, I drove into Dublin, where I parked up on an island in the middle of O'Connell Street, before hopping out and meeting a former classmate from Templemore, John McCarthy, in the Gresham Hotel. John had won three All-Irelands with Dublin and had been a substitute in the final the day before. After drinking there for a few more hours, I ended up falling asleep outside in the car before driving home.

When I woke up the next morning, the pain in my wrist was killing me so I went into Blanchardstown Hospital, where they confirmed I had broken it again and put me in plaster. I went back to Cumiskey's for a cure and was met by the barman's uncle, Paddy Delaney.

'At least you were drunk,' he said as I walked in with my arm in a cast. 'You have some excuse, but as for this gobshite –'

With that, Fintan appeared behind the bar with both wrists in casts. I burst out laughing and the piss-up continued.

# 15

# A wake-up call in Galway

When Mick Barrins left the Sub-Aqua Unit in late 1985, we had no sergeant and, of the group that had started in 1974, just Mick Carr and I remained. I began to think about taking over as sergeant. Although I had been in the gardaí thirteen years by then, nobody had ever taken me under their wing and explained the procedure for getting promoted. In fairness, up to now, I hadn't followed it up myself. I was too busy doing the job and drinking to think about a career. I soon found out that you couldn't get promoted until you passed the annual exam for each rank and then went for an interview.

I later realized that the best time to do the sergeants' exam was as soon as possible after coming out of Templemore, when everything you've learned is still fresh in your mind and you have a great chance of passing it straight away. With the next sergeants' exam due to be held in May 1986, I knuckled down to studying.

When the garda soccer team beat UCD in the third round of the FAI Cup, I pulled a muscle in my thigh and, in an effort to get fit for a once-in-a-lifetime fourth-round draw against League of Ireland team Derry City, I gave up drinking for a few weeks before the match.

Having been pulled out of the hat first, we forfeited home advantage to play in Derry's ground, the Brandy-well, so that we would have the experience of playing on a League of Ireland pitch and also get a share of the bigger gate, which could be put towards the cost of a pro-posed new garda soccer ground in Westmanstown in west Dublin.

There was a national debate about a garda team travel-ling across the border. When the Ulster Volunteer Force issued a death threat against the team in the week leading up to the game, the government was unsure whether to allow us to travel right up until the last couple of days, when Deputy Commissioner Eamonn Doherty persuaded them it would be fine.

On 1 February the team travelled up on a bus. Although I was still injured, our new manager, former Shamrock Rovers legend Mick Leech, rewarded my loyalty over the years and kept me in the squad, so I travelled as a substi-tute. Thinking that I would be able to study for the sergeants' exam on the way up and while we were waiting around in the hotel, I brought my books with me.

But with RTÉ television cameras on board capturing the atmosphere, Deputy Commissioner Doherty, who was from Buncrana in Donegal, joined us as we sang trad-itional Irish songs the whole way to Ballybofey in Donegal, where we stayed in a hotel ahead of our short trip across the border the next day.

As the game was being played in the Catholic Bogside, the RUC didn't really get involved in security until the last minute. Instead, we were met at the border and escorted to the venue by local republican sympathizers. They were delighted to be bringing 'their' Irish police across the border and into the nationalist stronghold and cradle of the Troubles: the garda team playing on their turf was like giving two fingers to their Protestant neighbours in the Fountain, as well as to the British establishment. For us, it was an opportunity to play soccer at the highest level in Ireland and we felt we were doing our little bit to show people that Northern Ireland wasn't all about the Troubles.

We received a huge reception when we ran out on the pitch to warm up. Over 14,000 fans turned up in the Brandy-well with over 1,000 gardaí having made the journey from all over Ireland to see us play. Our wives were sitting in the stand with local journalist and civil rights campaigner Nell McCafferty, who took them on a tour of Derry before the game and treated them to a few pre-match drinks.

Managed by the legendary Noel King, Derry City had exotic new signings Owen Da Gama from South Africa and Nelson da Silva from Brazil on display that day and were simply too strong for us. With around twenty minutes to go we were being beaten 4–0 when Mick Leech turned to the bench and asked me if I wanted to go on.

'Mick, I'll go on in the nude if you want!' I answered.

At the same time the legendary Brendan Bradley, the all-time leading goalscorer in the League of Ireland, was getting ready to come on for Derry. I had followed Bradley's progress for years and told him so as I shook hands with him as we stood on the sideline waiting to go on. I went on at right back and recall one of our players, Eddy

Hyland, wanting to know if there were to be any tactical changes for the last twenty minutes.

'What's the story, Tosh?' he roared over to me.

'What's the story? The story is that we're getting beaten four—nil and enjoy the rest of the game,' I said.

Within a couple of minutes of coming on, Brendan Bradley had banged in another goal for Derry.

My major contribution to the game was upending Nelson da Silva with a tackle within minutes of coming on. When the referee ran over to give me a yellow card, I was sprawled on the ground beside the writhing da Silva.

'Sorry, Ref, I didn't mean it,' I said. 'I wasn't warmed-up properly!'

I found out later on from Paddy Daly, a guard based in Mountjoy and an FAI referee's inspector, that the ref almost burst out laughing and had to put the card back into his pocket and turn away from me.

After the match we were brought in for food and drinks and were merry by the time we arrived back to Ballybofey on the bus that evening.

Although there was little studying done that weekend, I stopped drinking again in May to do the sergeants' exam, where I remember seeing a garda across the hall in the RDS taking out from his breast pocket a piece of paper with something written on it, which he had folded up into a concertina. He later went on to a senior job.

I passed the exam with flying colours but, like most semi-state or state jobs, passing the exam, or even the interview afterwards, had little bearing on whether you got the job. You were only promoted if you had a bit of pull somewhere higher up the chain of command. Before the interview, a sergeant wrote his opinion of you as a candidate. Back then I was naïve and didn't understand how it worked but now I know that all it takes is a line saying 'I don't think this man is ready' scribbled on a piece of paper for your application to be postponed until the following year, when it would be considered again. Alternatively, a phone call to someone on the interview panel the night before from a friend higher up the ladder could ensure a man was promoted.

Shortly before my sergeants' interview I was in Waterford, dropping Thomas down to stay with my parents as Susan and I were going to the World Cup Finals in Mexico. That day I was out drinking in Tramore when a local who knew that I was a garda tapped me on the shoulder and told me there was a fight out on the street.

I walked out the front door to see a man standing on the roof of a parked car. A young Waterford lad jumped up on the bonnet to challenge him but was met with a boot that saw him crash to the road and split his head off the ground. I ran over and challenged the assailant but he took off as a local girl, who said she was a nurse, leaned over the injured youngster.

'We can't let him off with that,' I said to the bouncer as I flashed him my garda ID and gave chase.

Despite being dressed in slip-on shoes and white chinos – à la Crockett and Tubbs from TV cop show *Miami Vice*, which was all the rage at the time – I caught up with the attacker. Just as I had a grip of him and he turned to confront me, a big fist came from behind me and clattered him to the ground. I looked around to see the bouncer standing over me.

'Show me that ID again!' he said.

When I showed it to him again, he grabbed our runaway and pinned him to the ground, with me encouraging him to break his arm if he resisted. The bouncer, it turned out, was a judo expert.

Within minutes a crowd had gathered alongside us and a woman pleaded with me to let the man up. When I told her the story of what had happened, however, a man in the crowd drew a kick on the assailant but ran away when he saw the patrol car coming. When I was brought back to the station to make a statement I was grabbed from behind by a sergeant who thought I was being arrested.

The young lad who had been kicked off the car died shortly after and Michael Keenan from Coolock was later convicted of manslaughter. I never got any official recognition for my part in the incident. Despite having arrested a killer, when I went for my promotion interview afterwards an officer told me that I was not involved in 'mainstream policing'. I bit my lip and resisted the urge to tell my interviewer that I had been in more streams than he'd had hot dinners but when he told me that any garda could do my job I disagreed and suffered the consequences, remaining an ordinary garda.

After seeing Diego Maradona lift the Jules Rimet Trophy in Mexico that summer, I returned to Ireland in August, just in time for one of the worst storms to hit the country in decades. Hurricane Charley had already wreaked havoc in Cuba and Orlando before it hit British and Irish shores, causing at least five deaths here, setting records for the greatest daily rainfall total in the country and causing rivers to burst their banks.

In Dublin, up to eight feet of water flooded into homes when the Dodder burst its banks, and we were brought to Ballsbridge, where we spent the night helping to evacuate residents from their flooded homes in our little Zodiac boat. Some of the older people refused to leave, so we visited them during the night and ensured they were warm and had enough food and other supplies. Bray saw about 1,000 people evacuated by boat and hundreds of others either leaving their homes or trapped upstairs in them.

On my thirty-third birthday we were called out to Castletownbere in west Cork, where a Spanish trawler, the *Contessa V*, had sunk off Bere Island. Five of the crew of fifteen had drowned. On my first dive, I found one of the men at the wheelhouse with two life jackets floating on the ceiling over his head. I brought his body up onto the roof of the wheelhouse, where I found the buoys used to mark the trawler's fishing spots tied onto the roof.

Instead of swimming the ninety feet back up to the surface with him under my arm, I tied a rope around the body and attached some buoys. Then, as he floated up, I went back in. I found another body in his bunk down a couple of steps.

Later we heard from the survivors that a youngster on board had had an epileptic fit when the boat hit the rocks and wouldn't come out, which gave John Conneelly and me an indication of where to find the next body and we went back down to look for him. The trawler had three decks, and from the wheelhouse you opened a trapdoor and went down a ladder to the middle deck before going down another ladder to the bottom deck, where the accommodation was. Still using scuba equipment, and with the cylinder on his back banging off everything as he went down, 'Jasper' managed to get to the bottom deck and find the youth's body. With very little room for manoeuvre, he pushed the body over his head and through each trap door as I stood on the floor above, hauling it up with a rope.

After the other bodies were recovered, John Harrington arrived home to Castletownbere from Los Angeles and, as he had been used to commercial diving with the Dutch salvage crew, we dived on the *Contessa V* later and took the bell off it as a keepsake.

After an unsuccessful search for a body in Carlow in December, a call came to find a man who had fallen into the Eglinton Canal in Galway on the day before Christmas Eve. Only Mick Carr and I were willing to travel so close to Christmas, while John Conneelly, who was at home in Salthill, offered to assist us. I'd bought Susan a chain for Christmas and gave it to one of the lads to drop into the house on his way home, just in case I didn't make it home in time for Christmas.

When we arrived at eleven o'clock that night, we were told that somebody had seen a man enter the water and heard a splash a few hundred yards before the lock gate at Parkavera. Thinking we would have no problem finding the body, we agreed to get in immediately so that we could head home for Christmas, but we found nothing.

The next morning, with nobody to advise or supervise

us, Mick, John and I spread out on a rope in the water and moved closer to the lock gate, while a local detective held the rope end on the bank of the canal. With no way through the closed lock, I was confident we'd find the body when we got to the gate. As we neared the gate I was on the middle of the rope with John to my left and Mick to my right, nearest the detective on the bank. I noticed a trickle of water moving towards the lock but thought nothing of it until John suddenly disappeared and, still holding on to the rope, I was pulled after him.

On the left-hand side of the canal, a door about the size of a small fireplace had been left open, and with the water rushing through it at a constant speed we got sucked into it as if we were being flushed down a toilet. We hurtled down through a dark narrow chamber and within seconds my mask and regulator were ripped off and I bounced off the walls of the chamber before exiting with a splash. It was like being sucked through a water-filled slide. The force of the water turned us round the gate and we came back out into the inner lock on the other side of it.

Shocked but thankful to be alive, I helped John up the ladder. Mick, knowing something had happened, got out and ran round to help us climb out while the detective – not really understanding what was going on – was still holding the rope on the bank behind the gate.

John had a big bump on his head and was a bit con-cussed afterwards. Despite coming the closest I ever had to losing my life, I put the gear on again and got back into the water. But I only lasted about ten minutes before shock set in and I had to get out. We never found the man's body.

The next morning, Christmas Day, I was working in the bureau in Garda Headquarters when it hit me how close I had come to dying and I realized that if anything had been blocking the exit from the underwater chamber (which I had discovered went out under the pavement at the side of the canal), or if John had got stuck in front of me, we would have both drowned.

A sergeant from ballistics poured me a glass of whiskey and we chatted about the whole experience, after which he advised me to get my injuries looked at and got a photographer to record them. A couple of weeks later I heard that three British policemen had died under similar circumstances. As their system saw them tied together by their arms, they got stuck in the chamber and all three drowned.

After my lucky escape in Parkavera Lock, I knew that I needed a clear head to be safe in the water so, after that last glass of whiskey, I decided to pack in the drink for good.

# 16

# Running the diving unit

Much as a trip to the dentist can make you take better care of your teeth for a while afterwards, or a trip to the doctor can make you eat healthier and exercise more, my brush with death saw Christmas and the New Year go by without an alcoholic drink passing my lips. Susan seemed relieved that I was off the beer but she knew my past form and therefore wasn't getting overexcited about my new-found abstinence. However, having gone off the drink for various periods in the past, I didn't see any reason why I couldn't just stop altogether this time round. In addition to feeling safer and more in control on dives, I now had something else to motivate me: I wanted to do a good job running the diving unit.

Although I didn't get promoted after my interview in late 1986, I was now in charge of the unit, which sometimes made life difficult for me. I was now telling lads I had previously dived and skived with what to do, and when new recruits came into the unit I was responsible for their training, even though I hadn't received any training myself since 1974.

As the unit was still based in the Technical Bureau at Garda HQ, with the divers split between the ballistics, photography, administration and criminal records sections, I was getting to know more and more people and some of these connections made it easier when I went looking for equipment or transport for searches.

I became friends with a fella who was in an administrative position and was involved in lots of areas. As I had the use of a van for the diving gear, if I wasn't out on a search, this garda would get me to bring items used in evidence back to various stations after they were returned from the lab and were beginning to build up in the stores. I would hop into the van with a colleague and often spend two or three days delivering stuff to Wicklow, Wexford and Waterford, with both of us staying in my parents' house to save money and still claiming a subsistence allowance. (Upon returning from the pub during one such trip, one of the lads who came with me wet the spare bed in the middle of the night. The next morning I had to tell my father that the hot-water bottle had burst. Luckily, he believed me.) In return for being available to help him process used evidence, the administrative garda would always look favourably on the diving unit if we needed diving gear or equipment, so it worked in both of our interests. I was glad to have made a friend in a position to help our unit.

When the British ambassador, who was big into sailing, announced that he was going to visit Kerry, a request came in from a superintendent there for the unit to travel down to check his boat before he went out. Although a previous British ambassador – Christopher Ewart-Biggs – had been assassinated when a bomb was planted under his car, a few days later the heads of each unit in the bureau were handed a circular, signed by Deputy Commissioner Eamonn Doherty, stating that the request had been turned down. Not thinking much more about, I threw mine into the tray on my desk and forgot about it.

The next day there was uproar when the *Irish Press* carried a leaked copy of the circular and an internal investigation began to find out who had leaked it. They were able to work out that it was my copy that had ended up in a journalist's hands.

Every member of the diving unit was brought in to be interrogated by a detective from the murder squad, Hubie Reynolds. I walked into the room first to see Hubie sitting with his shirt open, his tie hanging off and the room filled with a cloud of cigar smoke.

'Do you mind if I open the window or do you want me to call the fire brigade?' I said.

'Don't be getting cheeky,' Hubie said, before eventually letting me open the window.

'Think about it now, Tommy,' he said as I sat down in front of him. 'What lad in the unit is under a bit of pressure for money at home?'

'Every one of us,' I said. 'We're all under a bit of pressure, but none of my lads leaked that document.'

The next day there was a report in the *Irish Press* about eight disgruntled members of a specialized section of the gardaí having been interviewed over the leak, which meant that someone had told the paper about the diving unit being quizzed.

The incident soon blew over. It was only sometime later, when my new-found 'friend' – the garda who was

involved in administrative work – was arrested for em-
bezzlement that we got to the bottom of it. The guy had
been selling information to the media. Apart from simply
stealing cash, he had run a number of scams, one of which
I was unwittingly involved in, because I had dropped off
goods to a private address in the naïve belief that the man
had legitimately ordered – and paid for – extra for himself
when putting through a bulk order for Garda HQ. During
all this a very decent garda had been forced to retire over
false allegations about missing cash made by the actual
culprit. I was lucky not to have been in the frame too – and
all because I was trying to cultivate friends who could help
the unit.

It was a busy year for us, with twenty-three bodies recovered from all over the country. In the space of twelve
months we took three cars out of the sea at Tarbert pier in
County Kerry, the first of them a murder-suicide when a
father had driven off the pier with his two young children
in the back seat. The father was taken out first while Aidan
O'Dea found the baby in the back seat in twenty-five feet
of water and handed her up to me in the boat. Eleven days
later the two-and-a-half-year-old was found miles downstream, on the shoreline between Kilrush and Killimer,
her body having floated out of an open window of the car.

I spent yet another wedding anniversary away from
home, searching for a missing youth in Courtown Harbour. A month later, I returned to Waterford, where I was
glad to be able to find the body of a former schoolmate's
son in the river Suir, so that he could lay his boy to rest.

A trip to Malin Head in Donegal to look for two fisher-men missing off the *Boy Sean* trawler was interrupted by a second trip to Tarbert after a man had driven in off the pier.

Unlike the previous men who ran the unit, I believed in giving the new lads experience, and on our second call to Tarbert I asked newcomer Declan Schutte, who had only done a couple of training dives with us before, if he'd like to get into the water. As we were searching for the car, I gave a rope line to three divers and put Declan in the mid-dle, knowing he would most likely find it. During the search, he walked into the car, found his first body and became one of the best divers in the unit afterwards.

The next day we drove all the way from Kerry back to Malin Head to continue the search for the missing fisher-men. After completing my deepest ever dive, of over 165 feet, off Inishtrahull Sound, we were told the bodies had been found washed up on the shores of the Hebrides in Scotland, 130 miles away.

Although I had managed to stay away from alcohol, per-versely I had begun to make my own wine in Garda Headquarters. I had two large cans stashed in my locker in the depot and, for six months, tended to them without ever touching a drop. However, when the resulting bottles won awards for the best white and the best red wines at the Garda Sports Day, I thought it was time to sample my wares and began to have a glass with my dinner at home. Soon, a glass led to a bottle and I was back drinking again.

When Susan won a trip to a spa in England with a friend

that summer, she left me in charge of Thomas. She filled the fridge with food before she left and all I had to do was mind him for two days. I brought him to the pub on the Saturday, where he wandered around as I sat at the bar and talked to the barman. The next time I turned to look, Thomas had vanished.

After a minute or two searching the pub, I realized he wasn't there and I began to panic when the cellarman told me that he'd seen a kid running down the street as he was on his way into the pub. I ran out into the street and around the block, searching everywhere, and finally burst into O'Dowd's pub around the corner to see Thomas sitting at the bar drinking orange and eating a bag of crisps with two old men.

Although I got a massive fright I brought him back to the pub and continued drinking. When a customer later told me that I should 'bring that kid home and look after him', I almost attacked him and told him to mind his own business. Needless to say, Susan wasn't impressed when she returned to a fridge full of food and a story of how 'Daddy nearly lost me'.

# 17

# I am an alcoholic

Times were changing in the Sub-Aqua Unit and I soon found that I was the only one willing to drop everything to go on a search; and, with no sergeant over us, it was hard to muster lads for a dive sometimes, especially if it was at an awkward hour, or on their day off. It would be a long time before I realized they had more sense than me.

In May of 1988, I was one of three garda divers who turned up at Dublin Port after a car drove into the sea off the B&I ferry. After buying a new car in England, a young lad was following his father off the ship that night when he turned left and drove up a ramp, thinking it was coming into the harbour. Instead he drove off the edge, went into the water in his new car and drowned. When I arrived, I asked a few questions as to the whereabouts of the car, changed into a drysuit, put on my torch and jumped out of the back of the van into the water. Within a few minutes I found the young lad's body and brought him up.

When the Republic of Ireland qualified for their first ever European Championships at Euro '88 in West Germany in June, the garda soccer team decided to organize a trip to see them play. As treasurer of the group for the trip,

I helped to organize some fundraisers and we sold raffle tickets to lighten the bill.

We arrived at our base in Boppard, dressed in Garda Soccer Club blazers and matching grey trousers made by the well-known Dublin tailor Louis Copeland.

As was often the case whenever I knew there was a big drinking spree coming up, I'd given up drinking for almost a month before arriving in Germany. But as soon as we got settled into our hotel, I threw off my blazer, ran down the road into a pub and ordered the biggest, strongest, stein of lager they had. The rest of the lads soon joined me and we congregated in a beer garden at the back of the pub, enjoying the sun as we drank our first pints. I was sitting at a table with Liam Dempsey and Tommy Kinsella when suddenly a young man in a white shirt and black trousers ran from the bar across the road and grabbed me around the neck from behind. In a strong Donegal accent, he began to shout.

'You owe me money, boy! You did a runner on me yesterday.'

I stared at him in disbelief as the rest of the lads looked on.

'I'm only after fucking arriving here and if you don't let go of me in the next two seconds you'll be fucking arrested.'

When he twigged the garda blazers he realized his mistake and told us that a few English fans with tight haircuts, one of whom looked like me, had done a runner without paying the day before. I asked him his name.

'Clancy,' came the reply.

In stereotypical 'Irishman abroad' style, I asked him if he was anything to a 'Furzy' Clancy that I knew.

'He's my father,' he said.

It transpired that I had met his father on one of the searches for the trawlers in Donegal a few years before and that his sister, Catherine, worked in the garda murder squad. After a heavy drinking session that day, I fell asleep in the hotel but returned to the bar later that night to be greeted and saluted by almost every customer in the place. Although I had no recollection of ever being in the pub, everyone was thanking me for buying them drink earlier that evening.

As we were based so far away from the stadium towns, there weren't many other supporters in Boppard, and while going for a meal the next day we came across the three English skinheads dropping their trousers in front of some older tourists in the area. The police station happened to be close by so we grabbed them, took them in and told the local cops who we were and to put the Brits in the cells to give them a fright. Later that night, the trio came over to the pub and apologized and we were the best of friends for the remainder of the trip.

On another day I was walking past the river when I saw a few Irish lads from Athlone stripping off and getting ready to jump into the Rhine, which had extremely dangerous currents. I went over, told them who I was and what I did for a living and that I didn't want people at home reading the headline 'Irish supporters drown at Euro champs'. I talked them into joining me in the pub with the lads.

We were a four-hour drive away from the first Irish game in Stuttgart, where Ray Houghton's header six minutes into the game saw us beat England 1–0, sent us into a delirious frenzy and fuelled our sessions for the next couple of days until we met the Soviet Union in game two.

I drank on the bus for the four-and-a-half-hour trip to Hanover, or 'Hangover' as we called it, and after a spectacular Ronnie Whelan volley sealed a 1–1 draw and put us joint top of the group, I walked up and down the bus the whole way home. The last match in the group stages saw Ireland needing a draw to go through, with Holland needing a win for them to qualify for the knockout stages. After a three-hour trip to Gelsenkirchen we were beaten by a late Wim Kieft goal and knocked out.

After drinking every day for the duration of the group stages, I came home from the European Championships in a bad state. I was off the beer again on 9 September, when someone rang me early that morning to tell me that Vinny Hyland, my first soccer manager on the garda team and former drinking partner, had died from cancer at fifty-two years of age. In between jobs, I had often visited Vinny at home and we continued to drink together up until about a month or so before he died.

A teammate, Billy Keenan, and I went out to Vinny's house on Kennelsfort Road in west Dublin, where he was laid out in his bed. Since I was used to dealing with death on a daily basis I wasn't at all fazed by a dead body: we were so close that I thought nothing of lying in the bed beside Vinny's remains for a few minutes as a shocked Billy looked on.

Although I hadn't drunk in a month or so, I came down
and had a glass of whiskey with the others in the kitchen
and it kick-started a six-day bender. Billy and I went into
the Black Swan – or the 'Mucky Duck' as we called it – in
Palmerstown before heading over to the garda canteen.
When we arrived, the Garda Band was marching on the
square as Commissioner Doherty and the Tánaiste, Brian
Lenihan, were talking on the square.

I walked over and told them that Vinny was dead. Lenihan remembered him and said that he had known Vinny's
father from the Garda Band. I asked if we'd be able to get
a few lads from the Garda Band to play at the funeral and
Lenihan immediately said yes.

Billy and I headed for the canteen and continued drinking. I continued drinking up to the night of Vinny's
removal to the church. I was well sloshed when I got up
out of bed in the middle of the night to go to the toilet
and fell into the bath and broke my nose. I woke up the
next morning to find the pillow covered in blood. I
attended the funeral that day with sunglasses on to cover
my two black eyes. (A few weeks later – as a favour –
Dr Pat O'Neill, the Dublin Gaelic footballer, held me up
against a wall and twisted my broken nose back into place.)

I stayed on the lash for six days after the funeral. I went
down to the garda ground to watch a trial match where
gardaí from all over the country were trying to make the
national team to play at the European Police Championships a few weeks later. When I got there, one of the teams
was short a player so, despite being under the influence, I
togged out and played. I had a great game, calmly spraying

the ball around the pitch as elegantly as the German legend Franz Beckenbauer; I usually ran around like a headless chicken but my reaction time was so delayed by the alcohol in my system that everything seemed to be in slow motion. My performance was so impressive that I very nearly got selected for the Irish team.

As usual there was a bit of a session after the game and I continued drinking for a while until, after six days of drinking, I walked home from the nearest pub on the Friday night.

When I got home, Susan wasn't there. She'd finally had enough and packed her bags and gone to stay at her sister's.

I woke up the next morning with a nightmarish hangover but the garda team had a home match that day so I went to play. As I was togging out, a colleague, Richie Garvey, saw the state I was in and told me I'd have to do something about my drinking. After playing badly in the game, I drove to Cumiskeys and after a week of drinking I had a Lucozade.

Richie set up a meeting with a friend of his, a trained counsellor who worked in the ESB, and when I met him, he asked me twenty questions, after which he told me I was an alcoholic. As the man had experience in dealing with alcohol and other addictions I accepted this diagnosis and felt better that somebody else, who knew what they were talking about, was confirming what I already knew deep down. I agreed to meet him in the treatment centre at St Patrick's Hospital on the Monday morning.

When I went into St Pat's that morning there was no

sign of the counsellor but as I was waiting I bumped into a face from my past, an older garda whom I had been warned not to drink with on my first days in Ballyconnell, but had done so nevertheless. I went into a small auditorium and sat down beside him to watch a short film which was all about a stag do.

As I was looking at the movie, it brought back guilty memories of my own stag weekend – how I had crashed my car on the way and left Susan in hospital with a broken collarbone while I went to the pub for a drink before continuing on to my own party. How Susan had to wear a sling on her wedding day and we had to change our honeymoon plans. Although I never met the guy from the ESB, and never went to a treatment centre for my alcoholism, I picked up a pamphlet on my way out the door that day that changed my life for ever. In it was a list of Alcoholics Anonymous meetings.

I decided to go to my first meeting in Trim, County Meath, the next day. All I was short of doing was wearing a balaclava in case anybody might recognize me. When I went into the room, somebody shook hands with me and told me I was welcome, but, having spent a lot of time in pubs and hanging around other drinkers, I thought they were hitting me up for a few bob. When I sat down, people began telling their stories. All the while I just sat there listening and judging them, telling myself that I hadn't done what they had done. Despite that, there was a feeling of recognition: I began to feel like I wasn't the only one with a drink problem and decided to go to another meeting a couple of days later.

Having checked the little AA book, I saw there was one closer to home, in Blanchardstown Church Hall, a couple of nights later, so on the night in question I headed off and crept in, still wary of somebody noticing me.

When I entered the room I saw a senior garda there from Garda Headquarters, a man I knew to be very sound. I was delighted to see somebody I recognized and also felt assured in the knowledge that I wasn't the only garda in AA, so I sat down beside him. After a few minutes of idle chatter, the people at the top table began talking about flowers and gardens and never mentioned alcohol once. I turned to the superintendent and asked, 'Is this the AA?'

'No,' he said, 'this is the Residents' Association.'

Having almost crept into the room in the shadows, I had now broken my anonymity to a garda superintendent, and in a mixture of shock, frustration and anger I ran out the door and around to the sacristy. After pounding on the door with my fists for a few seconds, a shocked sacristan opened the door to be greeted by me bellowing at him at the top of my voice.

'Fucking stupid bastards, telling me there's an AA meeting here! What the fuck are ye sending me down there for –'

As I roared at the bewildered sacristan, I knew I had about £300 in my pocket and out of the corner of my eye I could see the Blanchardstown House pub beckoning to me from across the road.

'I'm after telling everyone I'm in AA –' I shouted.

'Calm down,' said the sacristan. 'That meeting's up in Roselawn.'

I turned on my heels and marched to nearby Roselawn, where I burst in the door in a fit of rage and carried on where I'd left off with the sacristan by roaring at the guy at the top table.

He let me rant and rave for a few minutes and when I stopped he simply said, 'Well, you're in the right place now.'

I looked around the room and saw one or two people there I knew and began to realize that we were all in the same boat. Despite my ranting and raving, I felt comfortable and stayed for the rest of the meeting. I met a man called Gerry that night. Without ever officially agreeing to, we became each other's sponsor and we have been friends ever since.

Prior to going to AA, I had given up drink for various lengths of time, from a couple of days to six or seven months. But rather than just stopping drinking and going home thinking everything was all right, I slowly learned that I had to change my lifestyle in order to stay off it permanently. One of the first things I did was give up playing soccer, as training sessions and matches always led to drinking sessions afterwards.

I also knew that searches led to sessions in the pub afterwards so I started bringing the little AA book with me whenever we got called out and instead of going to pubs all over the country I went to AA meetings.

When I told one of the new lads in the unit, Declan Schutte, about the meetings, he encouraged me to go, even if they were twenty miles away. He would come with me for the drive and sit in a bar reading the paper and having two or three pints while I sat in the meeting. For about four years, the rest of the unit thought we were having affairs with women but one of the best things about AA is that it's anonymous and you don't have to tell anyone anything you don't want to. When I'd come out from a meeting, Declan would ask if everything was all right and that was it. There was never another word about it.

I began to reflect on my drinking and even started to share my story at meetings but was told that, while it was good to reflect, it was better to look forward rather than dwelling on the past. Somebody told me that 'if you look in the mirror for too long you're going to run into the wall'.

Having made up my mind to finally stop drinking, I also made up my mind to run the diving unit in my own way, the way I'd have liked it to have been run earlier. I decided to give the newer lads experience by letting them into the water and vowed to deal with things on the road, rather than running back and complaining to my superiors, and to do my best to get better equipment any time I could. As the year went on, the new lads got more experience in the water, and when a stolen BMW was cut up with a chain-saw and dumped in Blessington Lake in December, I used the search for the parts as a training opportunity, showing the recent recruits the various search patterns that could be used.

In February 1989 we were called down to Waterford, to search under Lismore Bridge for Aileen Daly, a four-year-old girl whose schoolteacher father had thrown her into the river from the top of the bridge. Having landed on the muddy verge of the river below, she'd clambered back out, leaving one of her wellies stuck in the mud behind her. Upon seeing this, Eamon Daly roared at her from the bridge to get back in, so she jumped into the river and drowned.

For the next ten days there was a huge search carried out, with the navy and Fermoy River Rescue called in as well as hundreds of people walking along the banks. The child's body was found eight miles downstream. (Her father was found guilty of manslaughter but insane by a jury at the Central Criminal Court that October.)

In April, with the Troubles still raging in the North, we were tipped off that the IRA had secured surface-to-air missiles from Colonel Gaddafi and stashed them in sealed lead boxes in Lough Fern near Milford in Donegal. The Sub-Aqua Unit was given the job of finding the missiles, which could be used to take down helicopters and even planes, in a massive lake covering 447 acres. We dived over and back across the lake for hours every day while the Army Rangers, the Irish version of the SAS, camped out in the woods at night in case the IRA tried to retrieve the missiles while we weren't there.

By now our accommodation had been upgraded to hotels and leisure centres and we stayed in the Mount Errigal Hotel in Letterkenny. Instead of propping up the bar, I played golf in the evening or went to the leisure centre.

Meanwhile, our wives and partners were at home up to their necks in housework and homework. Having said that, by now Susan was ready to pursue her own interests. With the intention of moving to a bigger property, we had put our house up for sale but after a few weeks passed with few interested viewers, Susan had a brainwave. Having worked in a childcare facility for the previous couple of years, she suggested we keep the house and turn it into a crèche. I encouraged her. So, when we found a bigger house to move to, while I was away diving, Susan went about setting up her own business.

After five weeks of fruitless searching in Lough Fern, we were called out to the fishing village of Downings, about twelve miles away, to search for two men missing off a boat there. After diving in Lough Fern on the morning of 2 June, we got ready to dive that afternoon in Downings in front of a huge group of onlookers, some of whom were staunch republicans and not too impressed with our search for IRA weaponry.

We launched our little dinghy from the beach and went out about two miles into a very choppy ocean until we found ourselves between the two reefs where the men had gone missing.

The conditions were pretty bad and, with two of us in the boat and four in the water, we were finding it hard to stay away from the rocks nearby. The dive ended without us finding anything but when we got back to the beach a local garda, under pressure from the crowd gathered on the shore, ordered us back into the water.

I explained to him that we had already dived in Milford that morning, having been there for five weeks, diving twice a day, and that the lads were tired. One of the locals piped up that he knew what we were looking for in Lough

Fern and that we'd find 'fuck all out there' and then the crowd started giving us abuse.

'These are not fish,' I said, pointing to the lads. 'They can't spend all day in the water.'

Although I had every intention of coming back the next morning, I then got so much abuse from the onlookers that I told them we wouldn't be back at all, and we all left.

Back in Letterkenny, I got a phone call from local TD Pat 'the Cope' Gallagher as I was having my dinner.

I explained the situation again – that we had a shitty little dinghy for a ninety-foot dive in terrible conditions – and told him that I wouldn't be going back there as long as I was getting abused. The next phone call was from a senior garda in Donegal, who put pressure on us to go back up and assured me there would be no more hassle.

When we got back up to Downings the next morning, a couple of lads from the local scuba club arrived with two boats. For some reason, I pulled a new green drysuit out of the back of the van and put it on, which made me a bigger target for the abuse coming from the shore. I ignored the jeers as we went out. We dived in three groups of three and I went in with Declan and a local man. The weather was still bad but under the water the visibility was good.

Within minutes I spotted a body wedged between two rocks. The three of us took off in the same direction but I was so riled by the crowd on the shore that I made sure I got to the body first and I brought him up to the surface as happy as if I had won the lotto.

Word went around by radio that we had got a body and

I put him in the boat and stood over him like Captain Ahab, holding the rope on the bow as the boat bounced all over the place on the way in. We were last in and, as soon as we landed on the shore, the crowd rushed over. Their attitude changed immediately. The man who had fought with me the day before came over and shook my hand. We were brought up to a local hall and given food and tea while another local brought myself and Aidan back to his house and presented us with two huge salmon, which he told us had been caught in the same spot on the same day that the two men drowned.

Despite having been in Donegal for over a month, I spent another wedding anniversary away from home when I travelled to Burtonport a month later and spent six days searching for a group of British students who had been staying on Íochtar Island. They had taken two dinghies on a day trip to Arranmore, but one had taken in water and capsized while the other boat carried on, its occupants unaware of their friends' plight, as the six people from the capsized boat were left clinging to it. One man managed to swim the 300 yards back to Arranmore to raise the alarm. The local lifeboat rescued a young woman but could find no trace of the other four.

When we arrived in Burtonport there was no accommodation to be found as the Mary of Dungloe Festival was on at the same time. Mick Carroll, Declan Schutte and I went to the Ostán Na Rosann Hotel and I told them who I was and that I'd been up there for the *Evelyn Marie*, the *Carraig Una* and the *Skifjord* disasters. The manager told me he had only one room left with two beds in it but said there was a spare bed in a room down the hall that had only one occupant if we wanted to see if he would give it to us. The single occupant was RTÉ presenter Derek Davis and he was happy to give us the bed, so we dragged it up to our room and the three of us stayed there for the duration of the search.

On the day we arrived, a diver from the local Sheephaven Sub-Aqua Club had found one of the bodies and, using the Arranmore Ferry to tow over twenty divers on a line behind it, we found the other three in the next four days.

Having spent a lot of time drinking with the fishermen on my previous visits to Dungloe for inquests and searches, meeting up with them all again was the first real test of my sobriety. On the day before we found the last body, a wedding party arrived onto the island with some of the children of the men lost on the *Carraig Una* and *Evelyn Marie* aboard.

I was introduced to them all and, with the diving unit all invited to the wedding, I watched as some of the lads danced around in wellies and wetsuits that evening. But myself and Declan and a local diver, whose brother was a garda in Dublin, got into a boat and made our way from Arranmore back to the mainland and went home. By the time we got back to our new base in Santry, I had been sober for a year, my longest stretch ever.

# 18

# Sergeant Lavery, at last

Early in 1990 a working party was formed to look into health and safety in the diving unit. On a four-man committee, I was the only one who knew anything about diving. After some research into various search units in other countries, I wrote a report on what I thought should be done to bring the garda unit up to scratch, including sending divers on courses with the Association of Police Officers in Strathclyde and Fort William in Scotland and even the NYPD divers in New York.

I also said we needed upgraded equipment including better boats and more suitable means of transport to the searches, and I drew up various guidelines for each type of search pattern, explaining how they should be employed. When I mentioned the fact that the unit had been operating without a sergeant for the past four years, my comment was skated over and we moved on to something else.

Although I had given up playing soccer I was still an avid fan, so when Ireland qualified for our first ever World Cup Finals in Italy in 1990 I was among the first on the plane. It was a fantastic trip – particularly because I ended up as a sort of sub-agent for the travel company that I always booked my trips with, and helped organize tickets for the Romanian and Italian games when Ireland got out of the group stage. I went to the game against Romania with thousands of pounds in a bag wrapped around my stomach and have a vivid memory of trying to hold on to it as David O'Leary scored the penalty that put us through to the quarter-final meeting with Italy.

Once I had secured 300 tickets for the Ireland–Italy game, I took a taxi straight to the Vatican, where my colleague Mick Carroll's brother, a priest there, hid them in a little attic in his bedroom. As I doled out the tickets to the fans later they began to call me Paddy Schillaci, after the Italian striker Toto Schillaci.

I can still see the tears running down Thomas's face when the same Schillaci scored after thirty-eight minutes and ended our World Cup dream. I had already had my victory, though. Throughout the whole thing, I had not touched a drop of alcohol. As I sat in St Peter's Square afterwards, I noticed a drunk lying flat out across a doorstep and got Susan to take a photo as I stood beside him. That photo is a constant reminder of where I could have ended up if I'd continued drinking.

By chance, a few minutes later Superintendent Barney Curran from Dungarvan walked across the square with Fianna Fáil minister Ray Burke and a sergeant from Dublin Castle. They had been in Italy to help the local cops police the Irish fans but, unlike the English fans, the Irish supporters never gave the Italians a minute's trouble.

The superintendent walked over and shook hands with me.

'Well done, Tosh, you're on the list!'

'What do you mean? What list?'

'The promotion list. It came out yesterday and your name is on it.'

Having passed the sergeants' exam four years earlier, I had gone for interview every year since then but had been passed over. Now I was finally going to be a sergeant.

It had taken Susan a long time to believe I was going to stay away from alcohol. She had seen me give it up before – even for almost a year in 1987 – only to go back on it the first wedding, funeral or long weekend that came along. Slowly but surely she started to see that I was serious and, although we were no longer going out to the pub together, our relationship bloomed and we began talking about having another child.

After trying for a while, Susan and I started looking into adopting a second child. After a very long process of filling in forms, doing interviews and going through various checks and vetting procedures, we were finally offered a beautiful little baby boy from Dublin.

Our son Philip arrived home shortly after Christmas in 1990. He was just five months old. On the night he arrived he cried for the first couple of hours but, with big brother Thomas doting on him straight away, he slotted right into our little family and he hasn't given us the least bit of trouble since.

When it came time to christen Philip in early 1991 I remembered how I had been drawn back to drinking by occasions such as funerals and weddings and feared that the christening might do the same. In an effort to fill the gap left by soccer and to stay fit, I had taken up cycling the year before. I began to race on the amateur scene, and although I got hammered in my first year I was slowly beginning to improve. So, having ridden the first two stages of the Rás Laighean three-day stage race on the weekend of Philip's christening, I stood in Blanchardstown church dressed in a suit and tie, but with my cycling shorts on under my trousers and even my cycling socks on under my black formal socks. As soon as the ceremony was over and the others headed for the reception, I left for Dunboyne and rode the final stage of the race.

Afterwards, I threw my bike in the boot and drove back to the pub, just in time for the meal. Although it was selfish, and probably made me look bad in front of my family, for me christenings had previously been associated with drinking, and by going to the race and using up a lot of nervous energy I had lowered the risk of drinking associated with standing around at a bar before the meal.

When I finally got promoted to sergeant in 1991, I was forced to leave the diving unit in a compulsory move for promoted gardaí known as 'cross-fertilization' by the officers and 'bullshit' by the lower ranks. I was supposed to go to Garda Control in Harcourt Street but instead ended up as a sergeant in the fines office for three months.

On my first day, the inspector told me that they'd had a bit of an internal problem in the office and that there was an investigation going on into missing money. With the previous sergeant put in charge of the investigation crew, I was put in charge of the incoming fines, which would arrive into the office every day by post. In an archaic system of handwritten fines and summons numbers, checkers would go through all the post during the day and I'd have to go round them every evening and put the money in the safe and do the bank run the next morning.

I was now training to ride my first FBD Milk Rás, an eight-day international stage race around Ireland, and I used to cycle into the fines office. While the previous sergeant would get an armed escort to the bank in the mornings, I'd stuff the money under my cycling gear, ride into the bank and go training for an hour before returning to the office. As there were no showers in the building, I'd simply strip off afterwards and wash myself in the sink of the gents toilets.

I also had to deal with complaints and excuses at the counter but, unlike some of my colleagues, I had no real interest in summonsing people and if the excuse was any way good at all, I'd let them off.

It soon became apparent how easily money could go missing in the fines office. Letters would arrive with traffic fines with strict instructions not to issue a receipt as the person didn't want their husband or wife to find out they'd been caught speeding or parked illegally.

When the investigation finished two gardaí were dismissed. I felt sorry for the female garda as she had a young family at home and was getting very little support from her husband, who was also a garda and an active drinker.

Towards the end of the year I returned to the diving unit in Santry as Sergeant Lavery. The unit had moved from the

Technical Bureau to Santry as we were told there would be more space there for our equipment. In reality we were just given a bigger shed and were now attached to Santry District Detective Unit. Although we were based in Santry, however, our budget still came from Garda Headquarters so the inspectors in Santry didn't really know what to do with us. When we weren't diving we did land searches and were also armed whenever we had to help out with escorts or patrols.

One of my first jobs as sergeant was the search for the three missing crew members of the container ship MV *Kilkenny* when it sank in Dublin Bay on 21 November. On its way in from Holland, the *Kilkenny* was supposed to come into port by following a shipping lane that involved making a right-angle turn towards a berthing spot in Dublin Port. Instead, they decided to cut the angle and take a short cut diagonally across the lane, resulting in a collision with a bigger container ship, the *Hasselwerder*, as it was leaving the port. While the *Hasselwerder* suffered no more than a dented bow, the *Kilkenny* gradually listed onto its side. Eleven of the crew managed to escape by jumping or falling into the water, but three were trapped inside and drowned.

The Dublin Port Authority activated its emergency plan but doing so meant our passage to the water was blocked by fire engines, VIPs' cars and other vehicles. When we got to the *Kilkenny* it was on its side, with the top half sticking out of the water. I jumped up onto it, pulled open a hatch and looked down to see a body floating below me. I was so keen to get him out, I jumped in, ripping my new drysuit in the process and rendering it useless against the cold seawater. I grabbed the man and pulled him onto the side of the ship, where a red Sikorsky rescue helicopter from Dublin airport had landed. I handed the body over to the crew of the chopper, who flew it in to the ambulances on the shore. I later found out that it was the body of the chief officer, P. J. Kehoe.

Firemen were brought onto the ship by another little boat and made by their superiors to stand on the top half with no life jackets on. Given instructions to cut the ship with lasers, they were afraid to use their equipment for fear of causing an explosion as nobody knew what was in the containers the ship was carrying. As I passed by on my way back into the water, one of them called me over.

'Can you get us off here quick?' he asked, so I put them into our boat and sent them back to the shore.

John Conneelly went down ahead of me shortly after, and after swimming in along a corridor he pushed back a door to find the body of Dave Harding, the boatswain, behind it.

Many more lives would have been lost if it hadn't been for twenty-nine-year-old Dubliner Dessie Hayes. With most of the crew asleep in their bunks when the collision happened, he climbed down all the ladders and went around all of the bunks waking everyone up. Unfortunately, his body was never found.

If the accident had happened eight minutes later the *Kilkenny* would have hit the B&I ferry with 250 passengers on board.

*

December saw the newly monikered Garda Underwater Unit called to County Westmeath after a boat overturned on Lake Derravaragh. Three duck shooters from Dublin were missing. With no indication of where their boat had overturned, the whole lake, measuring six miles long and two and a half miles wide and with a maximum depth of almost seventy feet, had to be searched.

The army dug a roadway to the edge of the lake and set up huge marquees at the lakeshore. As the sergeant in charge of the operation, I soon found myself at the head of what was beginning to look like a war zone, with army and navy divers, dozens of onlookers and some of the Irish media swarming around the lake.

The difference between the army or navy divers and the garda divers was that they would all be huddled in a corner while their officers made the decisions for them. If somebody in the unit disagreed with my decision they could object, but there was no speaking back to an army officer, even if you were afraid for your life getting into a lake to look for a dead body.

I assembled all the eighty or so divers one morning, and what I said was aimed specifically at those army officers: 'I just want to explain something before we start,' I said. 'This is not a military exercise. We don't know where the boat overturned in this lake. You will start off in twenty feet of water but you could end up in one hundred feet. Visibility under the water is bad. There are three dead men out there somewhere. This is not like anything you've been used to before. Psychologically, it's not the same as sports diving. Your head will take over.

Do not feel under any pressure to dive if you don't want to dive.'

Two of the army lads came to me after two days and told me they couldn't handle it and were going home.

The body of one of the men was found floating at the shoreline on the far side of the lake with a load of plastic decoy ducks wrapped around him, while a second body was found on the bank with two hunting dogs, one dead and one alive, nearby.

The sister of the third missing man, Philip Moffatt, then put out a radio appeal for more divers to help in the search and pretty soon there were almost a hundred of us, some from as far away as England and Scotland, on the shore 'ready' to dive. As the search went on, the media presence intensified and people came to the lake to provide food for those searching. The place got so crammed with divers and would-be divers that some of the locals used to come out from the nearby pubs just to get a free dinner at the lake before going back on the beer.

Although I was in charge of the operation, I couldn't let go of the diving and ended up getting into the water myself. At one point we had twenty-six boats lined up across the lake with divers hanging onto scaffolding poles on ropes behind them as we slowly got towed over and back.

We were there for three weeks, carrying out a search on Christmas Eve before taking a two-day break for Christmas. We also went back for another week at the end of January 1992. Even with almost a hundred divers on duty in Lake Derravaragh for some of that search, we didn't find Philip Moffatt's body.

That search was the largest I was ever on. I'm still not sure why it captured both the media's attention and the concern of army, navy and garda management to the extent that it did. But if there's one thing to learn from it, it is that proper training is crucial in these situations. Having a hundred divers in the water was of no benefit when many of them didn't know what they were doing or, just as bad, were simply terrified. I firmly believe that some of those civilian divers had their eyes closed in the water, for fear of what they might see.

In the end, Philip Moffatt's body surfaced in May when the water warmed up. There are a lot of old wives' tales about the rising of bodies and how long it takes to find somebody who has drowned. The truth is that there is no such timeline and it depends on the temperature of the water as well as whether the person has a full stomach or has alcohol in them. If the water is cold, a body is more likely to stay submerged for longer. In warmer conditions there is usually a better chance of a body coming to the surface more quickly, as the food consumed begins to form gases inside which help float it to the top. Of course, bodies also get trapped or caught underwater and they are never going to come to the top no matter how long you wait.

Just a day after we left Derravaragh for the second time, at the end of January 1992, we were sent to south County Dublin to search for evidence at the Motor Yacht Club in Dun Laoghaire where a disabled pensioner, Johnny Shortall, was murdered. Having stolen a dinghy and broken into various boats along the harbour, somebody had broken into the club itself and battered the sixty-six-year-old to death as he lay sleeping on a couch and then stolen £600 in cash and ten cans of beer from the club bar.

We knew that whoever had broken into the boats had killed the man, so we checked all those that were broken into and dived for any evidence that might be under the water. On one of those dives we found a window that had been knocked from the wheelhouse of one of the boats and that happened to have a thumbprint on it. A man was arrested and was subsequently tried, convicted and sentenced to ten years for manslaughter.

A week or so later we were brought to a lake in Lough Rea in County Galway to look for a missing woman. Sitting in the boat across from me was a civilian diver with sweat running down his mask. He wasn't sweating because he was sick from the waves bouncing the boat across the lake; the conditions were near perfect and the lake was as flat as a piece of glass. And he wasn't sweating because he was hot; it was minus two degrees outside. He was sweating in fear – fear of what he might see under the water. To this day I cannot understand how we did not find her body. The water was so clear that I even found a golf club on the lake bottom.

# 19

# The people left behind

It had taken nearly two decades but finally there was some progress in how we were trained and equipped. Following the introduction of health and safety regulations and my report into safety in the diving unit, we began to get better gear. Sub-aqua clubs all over the country still had much better equipment and much better boats but we finally got a new truck with compartments in it for our diving gear and a little dry room in the back to get changed in.

Still, whenever we needed to buy anything we had to go through the rigmarole of filling in forms and waiting for them to be assessed before ordering the gear and then waiting for the invoice to be paid and stamped before we could collect it. This procedure was no use to us if we lost or damaged equipment during a dive, and it forced me to be creative.

In an effort to cut the red tape I went to the dive shop where we bought our supplies and opened a number two account with the owner. Whenever we ordered something, I'd tell him to add a few quid extra on the invoice and put the money left over into a second account so that we would have a few bob behind the counter if we needed replacement kit in a hurry.

I found another good time to get better equipment was towards the end of the year, after the budgets were totted up. A colleague from Garda Headquarters, who knew the efforts I had to make to get a bit of equipment, used to let me know whenever there was extra money in the kitty that was to due be sent back to the Department of Justice at the end of the financial year. He'd tell me to send in a few invoices, so I'd go and order safer cylinders with spare octopus regulators on them for buddy breathing, drysuits, or whatever we needed. I'd get the receipts from the shop and shoot them in at Christmas and our new gear would be delivered in January.

New recruits continued to come in as others went out, and, with the new emphasis on health and safety in the unit, when we weren't searching for bodies or evidence we did training dives and boat handling and radio courses with the new lads. We even began to go on proper dive courses at the Fort William Underwater Centre in Scotland – one of the world's best diving training facilities.

As I had sent all my log books and dive sheets to Scotland in 1987 and already received a Dive Contractor and Part IV certificate – an internationally recognized diving standard from the British Health and Safety Executive, allowing me to work internationally if required – I let the other lads go first.

Apart from searches, now we were doing security at various events. When the Swedish Royal couple visited, we searched for mines underneath a ferry that they were to use. We also patrolled around Lansdowne Road for Republic of Ireland soccer matches, the Progressive Democrats' party conference in Waterford and secured tunnels and sewers underneath Dublin Castle for various government meetings and state visits.

At Slane in May 1992, as Guns N' Roses played behind us, we rescued ten people as they tried to gain free entry by swimming across the Boyne, even though the whole area was fenced off, even had they made it across the river. Some of these would-be concert goers were weighed down with cans of beer in their pockets, which we threw away as we pulled them into our boat.

In another incident, I spent twenty minutes in the water with one arm around a teenager and the other holding onto a branch, with the river in flood, while the lads got ropes and enough equipment to get both of us out. John Conneelly even hauled a youth up from the river bed and saved his life but it was all in a day's work for us so there were no awards or Scott medals for him.

On the August bank holiday weekend the good weather saw half the country take to the beach or to the water and over a dozen were drowned in the space of a few days. We were called out to Blessington Lake, where four young lads who had been camping there took out a small boat that got blown away from the shore and capsized. We drew a line across the lake from where the boat left in the direction that the wind was blowing and got towed over and back and found them all. One of the boys still had his glasses on and also had four cans of beer in the pockets of his leather jacket.

In September one of Ireland's top financial executives went missing. We found his trousers in the water, torn, but with the button at the waist closed. I remember wondering how he could have got his trousers off with the button closed. It later transpired that he had run off with a girl, and had flown out of Dublin airport that day. We also searched for a solicitor from County Kildare who went missing. We were called out on two separate occasions to look for him but came up empty-handed. (A year later, the Salvation Army in England made him send a letter home to his mother to tell her he was alive and well.)

Despite the fact that I was now sergeant of the unit and had two young sons and a wife at home, I still never said no to a call-out and, more often than not, instead of standing in the boat or on the bank supervising, I wanted to get into the water and find the bodies myself.

Two days before Christmas I could be found searching a river in Ballinrobe for a murder weapon while Susan was at home doing all the Christmas preparations on her own. Four days after Christmas, I was in west Cork searching for a man who had parked his car in a car park and jumped off a nearby bridge. We didn't find his body until New Year's Day, which meant that I'd welcomed in another year on my own in some hotel room and had missed another family get-together.

Even now I was still acting like a single man, leaving home at the drop of a hat to go down the country, and maybe stay there for days or weeks at a time, leaving Susan to raise the two lads on her own. I took it all for granted.

Having begun cycling as a way to keep occupied when I wasn't drinking, by the summer of 1993 I was in my fourth year of competitive racing and as I was approaching the ripe old age of forty I moved into the veterans' ranks. Although I had been placed in a few races as I began to progress, my first win came in June of that year in the veterans' national road race championships.

The All-Irelands were held in Kilkenny and I got into the winning break coming out of Thomastown. Funnily enough, the breakaway group comprised two gardaí, an RUC man and an IRA man – the latter two crashing into each other accidentally before the end of the race. My garda teammate Adrian Byrne worked hard for me all day and led out the sprint where I managed to get the better of a former Irish international cyclist, Sean Lally, and beat him to the gold medal.

Cycling gave me a new focus and got me fitter than I had ever been in my life. I was lucky to have been taken under the wing of some very experienced local riders including Rás winners Philip Cassidy, Brian Connaughton and Seamus Kennedy. Instead of going to the pub on bank holiday weekends, I would travel around the country riding three-day stage races. I also still found AA a great help in staying sober.

When we were called to Helvick Harbour in October, the scene of the infamous *Claudia* gun-running operation that had led to the establishment of the Garda Sub-Aqua Unit, we were looking for teenage cousins Pat Tobin and P. J. Rossiter, who had been drowned while out salmon fishing.

As Helvick is nestled in the heart of the Waterford Gaeltacht, it was always a nationalist stronghold and had become a no-go area for the gardaí. Upon our arrival, however, we were treated as mere divers rather than policemen and the local community, knowing that we were there to help, welcomed us with open arms.

As we spent the next two weeks in Helvick searching for the two teenagers, the other divers would have a few drinks in the evening while I wandered around and visited the families of the missing men. This affinity with the families of missing persons was something that only really developed after I stopped drinking. When I was drinking, I never really thought much about the effect it has on others when someone drowns or disappears. I just went to the pub and drank and talked shit with the fishermen or whoever else was in there. But when I gave it up, I saw the people left behind, the families mourning their losses and how much it meant to them to have their loved ones recovered from the water. In turn, a simple shake of the hand and a 'thank you' meant a lot to me and to this day I have kept notes and cards from people all over Ireland thanking us for our help.

We found one body floating on the surface towards the end of our two-week search, while the other one was found floating near his uncle's boat ten days later, shortly after we left. As a mark of respect for the people who had looked after us so well, we went back for the second youth's funeral at the end of October.

On the night of the second funeral – which I spent walking around different pubs trying to get the lads who were drinking to leave – I got some indication of what it must have been like for Susan and others when I was drinking. When I eventually got them to come out of the pub, they fell asleep in the car as I drove home.

The next six months were fairly routine for the diving unit, if you could ever call what we did routine. But that spell came to a shocking end towards the end of April 1994, when the unit was called in to help in one of the biggest manhunts in the history of the state when Imelda Riney from Whitegate in County Clare, her three-year-old son Liam and a priest from a nearby parish, Father Joe Walsh, went missing.

At first the rumour was that Imelda and the priest had run off together but when investigators put the pieces together, and realized that a twenty-year-old local oddball, Brendan O'Donnell, had been seen with all three people prior to their disappearance, the search turned into a manhunt.

When we found the priest's car hanging perilously over Williamstown pier and dangling above Lough Rea, it was burnt out and had the passenger seat folded back the whole way. As some of the lads searched in the lake around the pier, I checked the car itself and found a little urn with some anointing oil in the glove compartment.

We found out later that Brendan O'Donnell had first taken Imelda Riney and her son to nearby Cregg Wood, where he'd raped her before shooting her and her child. The little boy was found buried beneath his barefoot and partially clothed mother in a shallow grave two miles from the village. O'Donnell then got an unwitting cousin to drop him at Father Walsh's. The fact that the seat was down in the car we'd found suggested that he had been leaning back, out of sight, while forcing the priest to drive at gunpoint back to Cregg Wood before making him kneel down and shooting him too. Father Walsh's body had been left in a forest drain in the same wood.

An Air Corps helicopter with heat-seeking equipment was brought in to help with the search and after eight days, and one of the largest operations ever mounted in Ireland, O'Donnell was arrested after a cross-country chase during which he tried to abduct a young student and hijack a local farmer's car.

When the arrest was made I let some of the lads go home. I was hanging around the corridor of Lough Rea garda station when one of the lads passed me on his way to buy clothes for O'Donnell as, apart from his boxer shorts, they had taken everything off him for forensic testing.

'Will you stand in there, Tosh, until I come back?' he asked, nodding towards the room O'Donnell was being held in.

I walked into the room to see a bearded pudgy man sitting opposite one of the gardaí's best interrogators, Bernie Hanley. Bernie smiled when I appeared in my long trench coat and wearing an old woolly peaked fisherman's hat.

'What you lookin' at?' O'Donnell inquired as he looked up at me.

'Well, howya doin'?' I answered. 'You're after doing a lot of running there. You're like Robin Hood there, running around the fields for the last eight days. You must be in good oul' shape.'

O'Donnell turned to Bernie and said, 'Who's this fucking head case?'

O'Donnell stood up.

'You're in good oul' shape there, all right,' I said, 'but there'll be no more cross-country running for you when you get to Mountjoy.'

O'Donnell stared and said, 'I won't be going to Mountjoy, I'll be going to Dundrum.'

For a guy who was clearly disturbed – and just how deeply unstable he had been for a long time would emerge as the investigation continued – he was remarkably shrewd about the workings of the justice system. At the time, it totally disgusted me that after what he had done he already knew he would never get the punishment he deserved. I'm still not sure how I feel about it, given what he did to those three people. He ended up dying in Dundrum a few years after sentencing, having had an adverse reaction to an anti-psychotic medication.

After the trauma of the events in east Clare, we were back to business as usual the following month. I was called to a security meeting ahead of the official opening of the Shannon–Erne Waterway, which linked the river Shannon in the Republic with the river Erne in Northern Ireland. When we were told that Irish Foreign Minister Dick Spring and Northern Ireland Secretary of State Patrick Mayhew would be opening the waterway by coming in from their respective sides of the border on two cruisers, I suggested we sleep on the cruisers in the days before as a security measure.

When the suggestion was dismissed owing to the cost of our subsistence while staying away from home on the boats, I pointed out that the Mountbatten bombing would never have happened if the gardaí had been on his boat the night before. My comment had the desired effect: a superintendent jumped up immediately and ordered that the diving unit stay on board the boats until the ceremony began.

# 20

# Dogs, diviners and psychics

The first time I came across water search dogs was in February 1995. We were in a beautiful little place called Martry Mill near Kells, County Meath, where an old man, James Tallon, had been cutting ivy off the side of a tree and been washed away in the flooded river Blackwater. When we found him, Mr Tallon was the healthiest looking dead man I ever saw in the water, despite being around eighty years of age.

I remember the search because of the sniffer dogs running up and down the bank, barking. They barked everywhere apart from where the body turned up, about a mile down the river.

I believe sniffer dogs on land are a good idea but they are a complete waste of time on water. Nobody will ever convince me that a dog can smell a body fifty feet down in a lake from the bank. Some people say dogs can smell oils from a body in the water, but what good is that if the oil drifts off in the current?

A month later we were called out to Carlingford Lough in County Louth when two brothers overturned their boat, the *Nicola Anne*, on their way in with a load of mussels on a bad night in March. I was training for another go at the eight-day Rás Tailteann, so I cycled the sixty miles down from Blanchardstown and met the rest of the lads there. The water was pretty rough when we went out. Across the water lay Northern Ireland, and as we searched a British security ship patrolled the far shore.

It wasn't long before we found the boat on the seabed, a little half-decker about twenty-five feet long, weighed down with mussels, so I knew the bodies wouldn't be far away. In my experience, whether someone went into the water off the bank or off a boat, they would be found somewhere within a 500–600-yard radius of where they went in, unless there were strong currents, and that the further you went away from the boat or the bank, the less chance you had of finding them.

We tied a buoy off the sunken boat to mark the spot but the weather was so bad it hampered our searches for the first few days and we found nothing. As we were coming up with nothing each day, the missing men's brother stood on the bank and begged me to search where the Mourne Mountain Rescue's dogs were barking, half a mile up the bank. I explained that I thought his brothers would be found near the boat, but for the rest of the week the dogs kept barking further down the lough and he implored me to go and search there.

I stuck to my guns, however, and told him I was staying with the boat, so we had arguments for the whole week, until the weather changed on the Saturday morning and we were able to put a long rope off the bow of the sunken boat and begin a jackstay search, slowly searching up and down the rope before moving in a circular pattern around the boat. I put in three divers, and on the third search they came across both bodies huddled together, dressed in yellow oilskins.

As I was dragging them into the boat, I looked over at the search dogs, and in anger shouted down to where their handler stood. 'Why aren't those mutts barking now? They're fucking barking all week, but they're not doing much barking now!'

I came into the shore and the brother who had fought with me all week came over and threw his arms around me in appreciation.

'I want to say something,' he said. 'I tortured you all week. I gave out to you –'

'You've every right to give out,' I interrupted. 'They were your brothers. No matter what people do when they're searching for missing people it's never enough until they're found. I know you were convinced about the dogs, but I've no interest in them. I don't believe in them. We just didn't get lines off the boat earlier in the week because it was too rough, but don't worry about upsetting me, I don't care if you tell me to fuck off. They're your brothers.'

While the rest of the lads went home, I decided to stay on that night and Susan and the kids came down and joined me in a hotel a few miles away. After a swim in the leisure centre we went for a meal in a local pub and the man came over and thanked me again. When we went to leave, our bill had been paid.

Apart from dogs, over the years diviners have also been called in to help the gardaí in their searches for missing people. As far back as 1975, when eighteen IRA prisoners escaped out of Portlaoise Prison, I can recall a diviner standing in Garda Headquarters in the Phoenix Park. Surrounded by a group of officers awaiting his input, he stood with two twigs wobbling over a map that was sprawled out on a table. When the sticks started shaking, his input came.

'They're on the move!'

Escaped prisoners, on the move? Seriously?

I've been in six feet of water with a diviner standing in a boat telling me 'he's in there' and me roaring back to tell him that I've looked three times and he's not. I've had diviners point out 'the exact spot' a body was lying in the water only for it to be found two miles upstream. After insisting they were right, I'd show them the current and ask them how the body got upstream without an engine attached to it. When it became apparent that the body was nowhere near where a diviner had said, they would come up with stuff like, 'Well, he stopped there on his way down.'

We drove forty miles one day to look for a gun used in a murder to be told by a detective that a diviner said it was '230 yards away'. I told the detective that he should arrest the diviner on the spot, because the only one who knew where the murder weapon was, was the murderer. As ever, we found the gun nowhere near where he'd told us.

Psychics, too, have had us searching for missing people in ridiculous places, places they would have had to be dropped out of a helicopter to get to. They too have stupid stuff to say, like 'He'll be found near a field with a horse in it, beside a white house.' If you look long enough along any river in Ireland you're going to find a horse in a field near a white house. When the body is found – nowhere near a horse or a white house – they say, 'Oh, well, he was there, but he moved on.'

In all my time as a garda diver no dog, diviner or psychic ever found anything for us. If they had, I would have had one in the unit because it would have made my life a hell of a lot easier. I'd have put them on the bow of the boat and let them lead me to everybody.

# 21

# In trouble again

In September 1995 I almost ended up at the bottom of the river Suir in my own home town when we were called out to search for drugs that had been dumped over a wall and into the river. Despite knowing that the current in the Suir was so bad that you only had half an hour's diving either side of the tide before it was time to get out, in an act of bravado I got into the water myself with a rope tied onto a karabiner clip on my waist while Declan Schutte acted as surface swimmer, holding the other end of the rope.

Underneath the bridge, the current began to take me around in circles and drag Declan away from me. The first indication I had that anything was wrong was when the rope began to go taut and, with Declan still holding on tight on the surface, it wrapped around me a couple of times and tied me to one of the underwater legs of the bridge. With no way of telling Declan to let go of the rope, I was pinned up against the concrete and began sucking the air out of my cylinder with fright. As my arms were tied above the elbow, though, I managed to reach down to my leg with one hand and grab the knife that I always carried strapped there and cut the rope before surfacing and ending the dive in shock.

At the end of that month, having by now let the less experienced lads go before me, I did my first diving course in twenty-one years. At forty-two, I was the oldest in the class in the Fort William Underwater Centre but all that meant was that I had the most diving experience. It was my first time using surface-demand equipment underwater and I couldn't believe how light and mobile I felt wearing just the helmet with my air supplied through an umbilical line to the surface rather than the usual cylinder on my back.

We were given various tasks to do underwater and even made a set of scaffolding, complete with planks and poles. I found the tasks all relatively easy, even if I did manage to build my umbilical line into the scaffolding and had to disassemble it again before I could surface. With the umbilical, though, I had an endless supply of air and could take my time as the others laughed at my mistake.

Though I was in my forties, I was now racing regularly on the domestic cycling scene and was the fittest I'd ever been. So the last thing I expected was any kind of health problem. That was in spite of having had pains in my stomach for most of the year. Typical man, I suppose.

After a routine garda medical I was diagnosed with diverticular disease, a problem with the bowel. It was nothing to do with diving and more to do with my drinking and the bad eating habits of my earlier years. It seemed like a fairly straightforward matter but after an investigative procedure in the Bon Secours in Glasnevin, I woke up in intensive care to be told by a nurse that I 'might' have cancer. Strangely, the first thing that came into my head was that I'd never be able to go out on my bike again.

As soon as I felt any way better, after about a week, I started walking up and down corridors and trying to get strong and fit. The specialist, Dr Parnell Keeling, came in every morning at half six to check on his patients and, upon seeing me out of bed and stretching on the balcony, after eight or nine days he let me out.

At home, I was determined to recover and began walking but got an infection and needed a second operation a week or so later.

Afterwards, I started the walking around the corridors again until Dr Keeling opened the door one morning, popped his head in and said, 'Mr Lavery, get back into bed. You won't cod me again.'

He shut the door and I spent a month in hospital.

In June 1996 I was on the way back from the funeral of a former Templemore classmate when I heard that Detective Garda Jerry McCabe had been murdered and Detective Garda Ben O'Sullivan had been badly wounded in Adare, County Limerick, while they were escorting a post office van. They had been rammed by a Mitsubishi Pajero, out of which two men wearing balaclavas jumped and fired fifteen bullets into their car from an AK-47 automatic machine gun.

I went home frustrated and angry. I sat in my kitchen listening to the radio when a story came on about firemen being stoned by a gang of youths as they took a body out of a house. I picked up the phone and rang RTÉ's *Liveline*.

With an active sergeant ready to talk about the day's events, they put me on the air live with presenter Marian Finucane, whereupon I let rip about Jerry McCabe's death and the renegades who were running around Ireland killing guards. I also told her that stoning a fireman wouldn't happen on my street as we all knew where our sons were and that it was the parents' fault.

Although I was angry and upset, everything would have probably been OK if I hadn't said that the Irish judicial system was a joke. I spoke about judges being chaufferdriven home and living behind electric gates and that they didn't live in the real world; that the criminals were laughing at us.

Within ten minutes my phone rang with various inspectors telling me that Garda Headquarters were cracking up and that I was in big trouble. A chief superintendent I'd had coffee with on the way back from the funeral in Templemore even advised me not to come in the next day and to lie low for a while.

Ignoring the warnings, I went in and was immediately called into the office of a commissioner.

'Sorry, did I disturb you?' I inquired as I saw him pulling up his trousers and putting on his uniform as I walked in.

'Shut up, you cheeky little prick,' came the reply. 'Look, I'm in a hurry. I'm going on an interview board in a minute. Everything you said yesterday was correct but we're in the guards. We can't say that! Now, go on out of here!'

That was the last I ever heard about it.

Three and a half weeks later, the nation was outraged again, this time at the shooting of crime journalist Veronica Guerin as she sat in her car at traffic lights in Newlands Cross, on the outskirts of Dublin.

During the investigation into her murder, a man who had been fishing in the Strawberry Beds alongside the Phoenix Park came across the carcass of a motorbike and went into Lucan garda station and reported it. Lucan happened to be the headquarters for the murder investigation and somebody phoned me and asked me to take a look for the rest of the bike in the river.

When I arrived with some of the lads, however, there was a tow truck already there preparing to pull the motorbike out.

'Hold on a minute,' I said. 'What's going on here?'

'I reported that two weeks ago,' said the man, 'and nobody did anything about it so I was going to take it out and do it up myself.'

I put on my drysuit and got in with a couple of the lads. That evening we took out the first bit of the motorbike, which had no wheels, no saddle and no petrol tank, and sent it up to the Technical Bureau in the park. Over the next few days we found two wheels half a mile away.

After finding the saddle, the petrol tank and the other big parts, we picked up every nut, bolt and wire we could find. We also found three or four rusted guns, which suggested the site had been a dumping ground for years.

The investigators interviewed a wide circle of criminals and slowly went through them until there were just a handful left. When Russell Warren was brought in, he turned state witness and said that he had stolen an English-registered motorbike with no indicators and no starter button on it. As the killers needed to be sure of a quick getaway after shooting the journalist, they had wired both onto them afterwards.

As we continued to pull nuts and bolts out of the Liffey, the motorbike was being rebuilt from a manufacturer's manual by one of the lads in the Technical Bureau. In his report afterwards, he noted that extra bits of wire and blue tape had been found and someone in the murder squad copped that this tallied with Warren's story. We had found the motorbike used by Veronica Guerin's assassin.

# 22

# On the way out

In the late 1990s, the diving unit became part of the newly formed Operational Support division at Garda Headquarters. A few years prior to this the government had wanted to cut the garda budget by a whopping fifty per cent, and as sergeant of the diving squad I attended the meeting where the cutbacks were discussed. Big money had been spent on forming the air support and the mounted units, and managing garda budgets by saving money would always get officers promoted.

I listened to officers asking for huge sums of money for computers and helicopters, and while some had budgets of up to half a million euro, the divers' budget was a mere €15,000 and I was determined not to lose any of it.

When it came to my turn to speak, I gave them a piece of my mind, even though I was the lowest-ranked garda in the room.

'I won't be taking any cut,' I announced. 'I have men going out there in treacherous conditions every day and even if we had the best of equipment, which we don't, their lives would still be in danger every time they get into the water. The only time that helicopter will get wet is when you're washing it.'

I went on about health and safety and the working conditions of my men and how important it was to help communities and families recover their loved ones. When the meeting was over, everyone's budget was cut back except ours.

When the divers, mounted gardaí, dog handlers and air corps were pulled together under the umbrella of Operational Support, though, things began to go downhill fast for our unit and it soon became clear that air support would always get preference, with the mounted unit a close second, while the dogs and the divers got little or nothing.

Until Operational Support came in, I had been responsible for the unit ever since taking over as sergeant. If divers were needed, the chief commissioner or assistant chief would phone me, often in the middle of the night when I was at home in bed, and I'd muster as many divers as I could to search for whoever or whatever was missing. If a van or jeep was needed, I'd contact one of the lads from the garage and invariably get one from somewhere. If we needed new equipment, I would find a way of getting some.

With the advent of Operational Support that changed and senior management got involved. Budgetary restraints meant that we were often delayed getting to jobs for a couple of days and, in some cases, we weren't sent at all. Most of the time we would be pulled off jobs because of a lack of finance rather than a lack of success. Excuses were made that we had to go to another job when there was no other job, and sometimes it felt as though turning up was just a gesture. I believed that every family should get the same treatment if they had somebody lost or missing, so this went against all my principles and after a while it got under my skin and started to fester.

Even after Operational Support came in, if we were tight on manpower, I'd get in the water on my own and do the job myself if I could, which sometimes got me into trouble. While some of the lads were in Boyle, County Roscommon, on a search and the rest were on a dive course in Scotland in 1997, I got a phone call saying that two young lads had drowned in the ninth lock in the Grand Canal in Dublin.

Although Phil Nalty had left the unit a couple of years previously and gone to the scenes-of-crime unit, he met me in Santry and gave me a hand to get my gear ready and put it in his van, while Susan drove across town with a weight belt that she had found under the stairs at home. We went over to Clondalkin and were met by a guard in uniform there, who told us that one of the kids had drowned when he got his leg caught in a shopping trolley underwater and another had died trying to save him.

Although the Dublin Fire Brigade had taken two bodies out, locals were telling us that another kid was still in the water. I went to the lock-keeper's house. He wasn't there so I got the key and closed the lock myself, letting the water fill up as I got in. I searched the whole lock but found no body, and with the water filling up to the top I rolled out and ran to open the lock gate again.

I was kneeling down on the concrete trying to get my breath back when somebody asked me why I was on my own. I told him that the rest of the unit had been called away. I barely registered a photographer taking my picture as I caught my breath.

The next morning, I was on the front page of the *Irish Daily Star* with a big headline reading 'Lavery left to task on his own'. I was out on the road, driving a superintendent to County Mayo. Just as I had finished reading the article, my phone rang with Kevin Donohoe, an inspector in Operational Support, on the line. 'Tosh, you're in trouble. The commissioner wants to speak to you.'

When I got back the next day the commissioner, Noel Conroy, had me in and read me the Riot Act about working on my own, health and safety, and earning bad publicity for the guards. I explained that I had no choice, that the rest of the unit was away and that there was possibly a drowned child's body to be found and I couldn't just leave it there.

As I walked out the door, I turned around and said, 'Sir, if it happens again tomorrow, I'll be doing the same thing.'

The commissioner winked at me and said, 'I've no doubt you will.'

After another working group was established by the garda commissioner in 1997, it was decided that the river Shannon and its waterways lacked a sufficient garda presence, so a brand-new patrol boat was built by Botnia Marin in Finland and fitted out to the specification of a similar patrol boat used by the London Metropolitan Police.

It had on-board communication with all of the garda stations and divisions along the Shannon as well as Marine

Rescue and any other boats. Despite my appeals to name it *The Brack* after the first sergeant in the Sub-Aqua Unit, Neil Bracken, the boat was named *Colm na Córa*.

The day the boat arrived for the new Garda Marine Unit that had been set up in Athlone, myself and a few lads escorted it to Athlone, where it was hidden in a farm barn until it was officially launched. After putting the boat into the barn, the farm owners came past on horses and I asked if I could get up on one of them. When I hauled myself into the saddle, one of the men tightened the girth on the horse but pinched its skin in the process and the horse reared up and threw me to the ground. I lay there unconscious for a few seconds as my colleagues looked on in shock.

When I came round, I felt a bit groggy so the woman of the house kindly let me go inside and sleep, which I since learned is the complete opposite of what I should have done after a bang on the head.

When I woke up, I drove to Waterford and the following morning I raced in the annual Hamper Race in Carrick-on-Suir, where I exceeded all expectations to beat John O'Brien from Carlow and former Tour de France green jersey winner and world number one Sean Kelly to win the race.

I was on board the *Colm na Córa* when she made her maiden voyage from Athlone into the Shannon and up through the canal. When we got to the North I kept sailing towards Ballyconnell and moored it at the end of Susan's family's land in Derrylin, on the far side of the border, where we took a photograph of the gardaí aboard a boat in Northern Ireland.

We were treated to a nice cuppa and sandwiches by Susan's mother. Then the postman called and took a photograph that ended up in the local paper, the *Anglo Celt*, the following week. That picture earned me a lecture back in Dublin.

While the family and I were on holiday in Spain in October 1997, the unit was flown by helicopter to Belderrig in Mayo when a currach containing retired German businessman Will Ernst von Below, Tony and Carmel Murphy and the Murphys' eleven-year-old daughter Emma got into trouble along the coastline and went missing.

At around half past five, with just an hour of light left, a search was mounted along the coastline with the Ballyglass lifeboat station, the Killala Coast Guard and local fishing vessels all involved.

An hour and a half later, shouts and whistles were heard coming from a sea cave on Horse Island, and when torches were shone into the mouth of the cave the reflective strips of life jackets could be seen in the distance.

Garda Superintendent Tony McNamara was part of the Ballyglass lifeboat crew and he called for a helicopter to pick up the garda divers in Dublin, while the Ballina-based Grainne Úaile diving club turned up to help in the meantime. Grainne Úaile divers Josie Barrett and Michael Heffernan swam towards the cave but with nine-foot waves slamming off the side walls Barrett was pulled out by local fishermen in a state of complete exhaustion before reaching the cave, while Heffernan was hurled against the rocks inside it and killed.

Sean McHale and Martin Kavanagh of the Coast Guard made repeated efforts to carry the garda divers into the cave in their inflatable dinghy but their boat was repeatedly tossed up onto boulders. When they finally got the boat into the cave they found the Murphy family huddled together in a crevice just three feet above sea level. They then discovered the bodies of Will Ernst von Below and Michael Heffernan.

With the Coast Guard dinghy's engine damaged, garda divers attached a rope to it and then Ciaran Doyle swam almost a mile out of the cave with the heavy rope, unreeling it until he got to where fisherman Pat O'Donnell took him on board his boat. Then the fisherman's boat began to tow the dinghy with the Murphys, the Coast Guard crew and the other garda divers, Dave Mulhall and Sean O'Connell, in it.

At the state's first marine rescue awards, a year and a half later, silver medals were given to garda diver Ciaran Doyle, while Dave Mulhall and Sean O'Connell received bronze medals. However, two other garda divers, Joe Finnegan and Kieran Flynn, who helped recover the other two bodies the next day, got no medals.

Although I hadn't been there, as sergeant of the unit, I told Commissioner Conroy afterwards that the garda divers on the job were a team and that all five of them should have received awards.

# 23

# Time to say goodbye

Through the 1990s, in my third decade with the Sub-Aqua Unit, the culture was changing in ways that I was not happy with. Perhaps the first small sign came on a job in 1994. That year ended with a search for a teenager from Wexford. Having been teased in school about a new haircut, he had hidden his schoolbooks under Edermine Bridge and neatly folded his buttoned shirt and jacket on the ground before jumping into the river Slaney. After a first search failed to find him and we finished up for the evening, I drove to Waterford while the rest of the lads stayed in Enniscorthy. I told them to get up early and be down there at half past six the next morning. But when I arrived at the river the following day, a civilian canoeist was coming in with the body and the rest of the crew who were supposed to be on the job were nowhere to be seen. I ran into the water in my clothes and pulled the boy in before laying him on the ground and washing his hair and his face.

The ambulance had already arrived before the rest of the garda divers turned up. To my mind, some members of the unit lacked a sense of urgency and failed to appreciate how important it was for us to do our best to find a body as quickly as humanly possible.

There was now a much quicker turnover in the unit. Some of the best divers from the second wave of recruits had stayed only four or five years before moving on to other areas of the force. As I had received no guidance in my early years, I tried to encourage the lads to better themselves and take their opportunities wherever they arose. Whenever one of the lads went up for promotion or wanted to move to another specialist branch, I spoke up on their behalf, but the danger of helping guys to move on was that I was leaving both the unit and myself exposed.

In April 1998 I let four of them go home from a dive to do the sergeants' exam. When a new diver, Joe McDonnell, had his mask pulled off him by the force of the water while being towed on a bar forty feet down in a lake, he somehow managed to surface safely but if anything had happened to him, I could have been in massive trouble for ignoring the new health and safety standards and not having enough divers on the team.

Another thing that began to irritate me was that it was getting harder to motivate the new lads to go on call-outs, and I felt that some of them simply didn't want to dive, even though that was their job. While sitting at the toll bridge on the M50 one day, I noticed a member's car in the queue ahead of me. To test my theory, I phoned him up and pretended that we needed him for a search. He told me he couldn't make the job because he was in Athlone.

Unlike most other branches of the guards, the diving unit was always on the road together. We worked with each other, lived with each other, ate and drank with each other and even fought with each other. Over the years I saw fist fights between members of the unit, and, although I was no longer hanging around the bar after dives, I heard of altercations and incidents at night when members had drink in them.

When I reprimanded one of the new divers in the Phoenix Park one day I was told to fuck off in front of an inspector. The inspector insisted I make a complaint to the management and submitted a witness statement, but when I filed the complaint – the first one of my career – all they did was bring the member in question and myself into a room and make us shake hands, which solved nothing.

Another member who was about to leave the unit called into my office and leaned over my desk with his hand outstretched. When I put out my hand to shake his, he grabbed me, pulled me towards him and headbutted me in the face. As he ran out the door and up the stairs towards the inspector's office, I fought the urge to run after him and seek my revenge – which I would have had no hesitation doing while I was drinking – by taking a few deep breaths and saying the AA's serenity prayer.

I saw fellas leaving the unit for understandable personal reasons: because they couldn't deal with dead bodies, or with being away from home – missing out on dinners and birthdays and special occasions. The nature of our work made it a stressful environment not only for the divers themselves but for their families at home.

As if I hadn't done enough harm to my own family already, in the summer of 1998 I started an affair. While I was drinking, I never had any interest in the women I met in pubs or clubs but suddenly, out of the blue, I had my head turned and for a while I thought the grass was greener on the other side of the fence. My head was in turmoil and I was living a lie at home.

At this time, when my personal life was in such trouble, the job was a constant, a reminder that there was always somebody worse off. A search we did towards the end of 2000 brought that starkly home.

We got a call from Sergeant Timmy McCarthy in Howth after a man had committed suicide by driving off the pier into the sea. The Howth Lifeboat had gone out to the site and two of their divers had pulled out the man's body. He was a fifty-one-year-old unemployed fisherman called Michael Burke.

When the sergeant went to the house to tell Mr Burke's ex-partner that they had found the car in the water, she was hysterical. Not simply because the man had drowned, but because she had just reported him to the local garda station for taking their nine-year-old daughter out of school without her permission.

I drove to the site, put my gear on and jumped in. When I searched the car, I found the little girl's body lying in the rear footwell and Sergeant McCarthy had to make another heartbreaking trip to the woman's house.

In February 2002 I got a phone call one lunchtime to say that a body had been sighted in the chamber of a lock in the Grand Canal. With the rest of the unit away on a search with all the diving gear, my arrival at the scene, on my own and without any equipment, was followed shortly by that of two fire engines.

A young lad jumped out of the first fire engine and, with

no thought for the family of the missing nineteen-year-old girl, who were in hysterics on the far bank of the canal, started shouting that he could see the body in the water. As an older fireman looked on, the youngster got a ladder and put it down into the lock before taking out a grappling iron from the fire engine, with which he intended to drag the body up along the wall of the canal and onto the bank.

Over the years I'd had the odd run-in with fire chiefs too keen to put their men into water without the proper equipment and I recalled one particular row at Hanover Quay after a fire officer told me that two of his men had been sent to hospital with hypothermia.

'How did that happen?' I asked.

'They were in the water,' he replied.

'Well, there you go,' I answered. 'You won't see us putting out fires.'

The young fireman was still running around shouting, and I asked his older colleague to get the young lad to stop. I told him I was waiting for some diving gear to arrive, and that when it did I'd recover the body myself and hand it to the firemen at the steps. That way, we would avoid the undignified spectacle of the girl's corpse being dragged up the canal wall and maybe even being dropped back into the water from halfway up, which I had seen happen before.

The older fire officer called a halt to proceedings while I phoned Rory Golden, the owner of Flagship Scuba in nearby Ringsend, who drove over with a drysuit and some diving gear for me.

As a large group of firemen and three local gardaí

looked on, I swam over, retrieved the body of the girl and brought her up the steps, where the fire service had a body bag and a stretcher ready and waiting. As I was getting changed afterwards, the older fireman, who turned out to be the fire chief, came over and acknowledged that this had been a more civilized way to go about things.

I spent New Year's Eve 2000 sitting in a boat. This time I was on the Liffey as a safety precaution in case anyone fell in on their way home from the fireworks display in the Phoenix Park. My phone rang and I was told that two young kids had fallen through ice into Hollywood Lake in Monaghan while skating.

I got some of the lads together and we were in Santry at six o'clock in the morning on the first day of 2001. Somebody asked if we could stop for breakfast on the way but I said no, as I wanted to get there as quickly as possible to assess the situation and be the first divers there so that we could get in and do our job unhindered.

When we arrived a few locals took me to the top of a hill that overlooked the lake, from where I spotted a hole in the ice with a spring in the middle where the water was moving continuously. We crawled out onto the ice on our bellies, pushing our inflatable boat ahead of us. The lads from the Boyne Fisherman's Rescue and Recovery Service were already out on the lake breaking ice but I knew that where the kids fell down, the ice had to have been broken already and so I headed to where the spring was.

When we got to the hole, I went into the water and almost immediately could see the body of a little girl lying on the bottom with her hoody still up. It was as if she was looking up at me. I put my arm around her and brought her up to the surface. I could see one of the lads about to go on the radio to say we had a body but, thinking of the two sets of parents on the shoreline, I didn't want them to get into a frenzy over which child it was and I shouted at him not to say anything until we found the other child.

I handed up the girl's body and went back down to look for the other one, which I found nearby, in about fifteen feet of icy water. By now we were equipped with body bags in the boat. Before we brought them in and their parents saw them I brushed the girls' hair and cleaned their faces.

They were brought into a marquee set up at the side of the lake. After saying a few prayers and having a few quiet words with the families, I went back to the van and was taking off my gear in the back when suddenly I was aware of another guard standing behind me.

'Are you all right?' he asked.

'I am. No problem. Thanks.'

The guard turned out to be a peer support officer; he had obviously sensed that something was not quite right with me afterwards and thought perhaps the recovery of two young children had taken its toll.

The support officer had good instincts. Something wasn't quite right. Although I was OK with the bodies, I had other stuff on my mind. My indiscretion had finally caught up with me and even though Susan had been generous enough to take me back afterwards, I had broken her trust; and now, rather than my home life taking my mind off my work, searching for dead bodies in the dark, murky depths had begun to take my mind off my home life. For me at that time, dealing with the dead was easier than dealing with the living.

A few months after the tragedy, I attended the inquests and spoke to one of the mothers, Mrs McAloon, outside. She told me how she couldn't sleep and kept imagining her child struggling in the ice. I explained that this wouldn't have been the case, that her daughter hadn't struggled and would have been in no pain. I told her how peaceful she had looked when I found her.

I later received a call to say that after our little chat the woman began to come to terms with things and was even able to make a poignant speech at the unveiling of a plaque in memory of the girls at her local school. To know that I had helped in some small way made me feel good.

When our first female diver, Oonagh Collins, got pregnant a couple of years after joining the unit, I thought of Susan and all the things I should have done for her during her pregnancy and tried to somehow make up for it with Oonagh. Although management wanted Oonagh moved out of the unit, I assured them that I had plenty of work for her. I tried to look after her by letting her stay in the office, making sure she got proper rest periods and even sending her home for a break when possible, insisting it was a health and safety requirement.

In March 2004, while I was at home with Philip and one of his school friends, I got a call from work. The two boys hopped into the car with me and we were met by a garda motorbike on the M50 motorway and escorted to the site where a girl had driven her electric wheelchair for four miles before heading straight off the pier in Dun Laoghaire.

I got my gear on and went down to the sandy seabed and started swimming around. When I couldn't find her, I went up a little further and found her sitting along the wall under the water in her chair. I unstrapped her, brought her to the surface and handed her to the lifeboat crew. I didn't know it then, but it was the last dive I would ever do as a garda.

A few months later, at her behest, I met the mother of the girl in the wheelchair. As a result of receiving wrong information about the nature of her daughter's death, the woman was experiencing similar emotions to Mrs McAloon. Again, I was glad to be in a position to put her mind at rest.

In June 2004 US President George Bush visited Dromoland Castle in County Clare for the annual EU–US summit. Around 7,000 security personnel were called in to guard Bush and other top officials during the visit, which lasted for just sixteen hours.

While the Irish army put tanks, jeeps and every tin can they had out onto the street in an effort to impress the Americans, various branches of the gardaí were also on display, with the divers busy checking the pond at the front of the castle while I looked on. As on previous presidential visits, however, the Yanks had a couple of jeeps with enough firepower in the back of them to blow the whole lot of us away and didn't need much more help.

As President Bush walked past me that day I shook hands with him and, with a couple of secret service men looking on nervously, I had a few words with him and made sure to hold his hand for a second or two longer so that I could get a photo as a memento of the day.

Back in Santry the daily grind was beginning to wear thin, and, although I could have had another seven years in the guards, I went in one day and retired. I hadn't envisaged leaving when I got up that day. Even on the drive in, it was just another normal day as far as I was concerned. But when I got into the car park, I just turned round and went home.

I had been falling out of love with my job for a long time and seeing an officer's car parked there reminded me of the red tape and unnecessary bullshit that had now become part of the job. I simply could not take it any more.

I went back later that day and filled in my form to leave the guards for good, after thirty-two years' service, thirty of which had been spent in the Sub-Aqua Unit. Before I left, some of the officers tried to convince me to stay but I had made up my mind and was not for turning. On 19 July 2004, I was gone.

Back in 1974, when I had trained for the first diving team, my instructor Brian Cusack had not been too impressed by my freewheeling attitude.

'You won't make it in this unit, Lavery. You're mad,' he had said as I passed my final diving test and was made a member of the Garda Sub-Aqua Unit.

As it turned out, Brian Cusack was wrong, although maybe not entirely. Thirty-odd years later, I was the last of the original crew to leave the unit, but for the same reason.

# Epilogue

When I retired I couldn't adjust to life at home. I was used to leaving the house at the drop of a hat and living out of a suitcase while Susan looked after the kids, got them to school, did the shopping and everything else that a good mother should do, as well as some things that a good father should have done. Unfortunately, that was something I didn't appreciate at the time.

From the time I joined the diving unit in 1974 I was always on the go and wasn't a great person to live with, especially when I was drinking. Although I was never violent or abusive, I could get up and go out the door and not come back for the day.

Susan knew how dedicated I was when it came to my job, though, and fully supported me until she finally had enough when I began my affair in 1998. After that, things were never the same. We separated in 2010. I take full responsibility for the break-up of our marriage and still feel guilty about it.

When I was on the road a lot in the early years I was getting paid overtime and subsistence and all it cost me was the price of a few drinks. At the time B&Bs were cheap and you might get the odd meal on the house or the local fishermen might pay for your drinks in the pub that night. Since my very first job, walking greyhounds in

Kilcohan Park as a youngster, I had always saved part of my wages. So, even though I wasted money on drink in the early years, by the time I had left the guards, after sixteen years of sobriety, we had bought and paid for two houses, which meant that Susan and I each had our own place to live when we finally separated.

Having retired shortly before my fifty-first birthday, I was far too young to be idle. I had always worked hard and I wasn't going to stop now. The year before leaving Operational Support I had taken a course in health and safety in the hope that I could become the unit's health and safety officer and, as I would be qualified to do all the training in-house, it wouldn't cost the state anything. With that under my belt, I was also qualified to work commercially in the same role, so I started my own health and safety company. I spent the next few years working in construction before the Celtic Tiger died and there were no building sites to assess any more.

I was two years retired when my phone rang at ten to four one morning, with a garda inspector on the other end of the line.

'Hello, Tosh; we have a car in the Grand Canal down at Cross Guns Bridge –' he began.

'Did you get permission from the superintendent?' I asked.

'Yeah, yeah, that's all sorted.'

'What about the overtime?'

'Tosh, that's grand, just get the team.'

'Well, I'm treble time now, you know.'

'What do you mean, treble time?'

'I'm retired two years now.'

'Aw, Jaysus, I'm sorry, Tosh. You're the only one I knew to ring.'

Shortly afterwards, in October 2006, when garda divers were searching for the body of Meg Walsh in the river Suir, I rang the superintendent in charge and left two messages offering my knowledge of one of the fastest-flowing rivers in Europe. I didn't hear back until, after a few weeks of fruitless searching, a detective superintendent I knew rang me from the riverside. He was a bit wary of a new sniffer dog the guards had involved in the search and wanted my opinion.

'If you want to find the body, the best thing you can do with that dog is give him a good kick up the hole, drive him into the river and see what way he floats,' I said, before explaining the zigzag nature of the current and that the only bodies we ever found in the Suir were floating on the town side.

Two weeks later, Meg Walsh's body was found, having surfaced on the town side of the river and floated downstream, while the dog ran around barking on a wharf the other end of the town.

I might have left the gardaí, but the job would always be a part of me.

Looking back, I might not have made the best garda if I had been on the beat while I was drinking but I was made for the diving unit and never missed a day's work. You had to be a different type of person to go into that unit: getting into water – an alien environment – every day; dealing with death on a frequent basis; leaving your family and the comforts of home whenever you got a phone call; never being able to make a plan.

In the early years, when I was drinking, I got a kick out of finding a body. Finding someone drove me on. I was doing my job and there was a fair bit of media attention on the new Garda Sub-Aqua Unit.

After I stopped drinking, though, I saw a completely different side to what I was doing. I was helping to bring closure to those families tortured by the tragic loss of loved ones. Indeed, on a couple of occasions, I managed to get to somebody before things went bad and pulled them out alive and well.

Instead of drinking alcohol and talking to the macho men at night, I'd have a quiet cup of tea and sit down and talk to those people left behind and I came to realize how much it meant to them that we found whoever we were looking for.

In 2011, seven years after I retired, I got a phone call from a garda friend asking if I'd give him a hand organizing a sponsored hundred-kilometre cycle ride with the Ballymun gardaí to raise money for Christmas hampers for local families in need.

I did a safety plan for the event and then participated in it myself. As we cycled around the east coast, through Balbriggan, into Drogheda and back, I chatted with everyone in the fifty-strong group. I knew almost all of them except one young guard. As I rode alongside him we got chatting and I picked up on his northern accent.

'You're from up around Donegal, are you?' I asked.

'I am. I'm from Killybegs.'

'Ah,' I said. 'I've a lot of affiliation up there. I was in the garda diving unit.'

'Yeah?' he replied. 'My father was killed in a fishing accident up there.'

'Was it the *Evelyn Marie* or the *Carraig Una*?' I asked.

'The *Carraig Una*,' he said.

I looked at him, guessing his age.

'Is your father's name Ted Carbery?' I asked.

'Yeah! How did you know that?'

'I found your father.'

The chap looked at me and nearly fell off his bike before turning to me and saying, 'I always wanted to join the guards because my mother told me that a guard found my father.'

We stopped near the graveyard in Duleek, put our arms around each other and started crying. I couldn't believe that, after all those years, I had met Ted Carbery's son.

A very well-respected young garda, he told me the story of his mother having a baby three days after the disaster. He was only one at the time. His mother had to rear the family on her own but eventually remarried and the family moved to Dublin.

I met his mother at a funeral shortly after Donegal had won the All-Ireland Final in 2012 and we had a photo taken with the Sam Maguire Cup. I hadn't seen her since 1976.

Although Mrs Carbery's husband was found and she can take a little solace from the fact that she has a grave to visit, dozens more families of missing fathers or mothers, brothers or sisters, sons or daughters, have nowhere to mourn and are still looking for answers.

In 2006 Kathleen O'Toole, a former Boston police commissioner, came to Ireland to head up the Garda Inspectorate. She called me in to talk about missing persons and made recommendations to the garda commissioner that more resources be given to missing persons and that a DNA database should be set up so that a body could be identified no matter where it was found or how badly deteriorated it had become. While television programmes such as *Crimecall* are helping to highlight the issue, missing persons is still at the lower end of the scale when it comes to garda attention.

Leaving the gardaí didn't change how I felt about the work I had been involved in. I continued to have a passion for searching for missing people. I have been involved in helping families of missing persons all over Ireland for the last ten years and eventually I set up a voluntary group called Searching for the Missing in 2010.

Whenever I hear that a missing person has been found now it gives me a great lift, as I know it brings closure to another family and goes some way to alleviating their suffering and feeling of loss.

Having fought with government ministers for a National Missing Persons' Day, our request was granted in 2013 and it is now held annually on the first Wednesday of December. Prior to this, with little or no funding, our small group held three memorials in Waterford, Drogheda and

Limerick and four pilgrimages in Our Lady's Island, for the families of the missing.

There is a lot of goodwill from the public when it comes to searching for missing people but the families just need guidance and a public voice so that their stories can be heard over the ever increasing clamour of everyday life.

Even though it's been eleven years since I left the guards I still have lots of friends in the force and from what I hear things haven't changed much in terms of resources. The age-old system of promotion, where the top 200 officers are promoted by politicians and then, for the rest, who you know is more important than what you know or do, is still in place.

As I write these lines, the Garda Water Unit, as it is now called, has just one sergeant from a possible four and the equipment needs updating, but I'm sure the budgetary restraints won't allow that. The simplest thing for a super-intendent to do to save money or cut out the danger is not to send you on a job. Like a child you don't let out to play, it will be safe but it will never develop.

I still go to AA meetings regularly and haven't touched alcohol since I went into that first meeting in 1988, twenty-seven years ago, with a man's body and a boy's brain. People may think the nature of my job caused me to drink – and, like most other walks of Irish life, there was a culture of drinking in the guards – but I saw lads doing it sober, without ever touching a drop.

AA educated me, though, and opened my eyes to the

real world. Going to that first meeting was one of the best things I've ever done. You don't have to be living in a cardboard box on the street to be an alcoholic. If drink interferes with your life in any way and it becomes unmanageable, then it's time to take stock. If you drink one bottle of wine at home and your kids come in from school to find you asleep on the couch with no dinner ready, then you're an alcoholic.

My biggest regret in life is picking up a drink and my biggest achievement was putting it down.

The greatest achievement in my career as a garda diver is that none of the unit died in the line of duty, although some of us came close on a few occasions.

As I've said already, I feel I was made for the diving unit so, when I left, I was like a fish out of water. Cycling saved me, though. It had kept me occupied when I stopped drinking and brought me to the peak of fitness. I still ride my bike almost every day and have friends in every corner of Ireland from the sport. I have also had the pleasure of seeing my two sons take it up. Thomas rode numerous Rás Tailteann events, was garda cycling champion a few times and represented the garda team in races abroad, while Philip represented Ireland at European and World Championships and in 2013 came within a whisker of turning professional for one of the best-known teams in the world. He may yet get to ride the world's top races.

A couple of weeks after I left the gardaí, Thomas passed out as a new recruit. He had obtained a business degree in recreation and sports management at Waterford Institute of Technology just one week before going into the Garda College.

At his passing-out ceremony, Susan and I stood alongside him and, as proud parents, we had our photograph taken in the exact same spot as my parents had stood with me thirty-two years earlier.

Staying in the diving unit for so long deprived my family and I very much regret the pain and hurt that my wayward lifestyle brought to them. Thankfully, I have a very good relationship with Susan and the two boys now and I hope to make a much better grandfather than I was a father.

Having lived out of a suitcase for thirty-two years, I still find it very hard to settle anywhere. Continually travelling to funerals and memorial services and visiting families of the missing means that I am on my own most of the time. But I'm living my life as I have always done, one day at a time.

# Acknowledgements

They say you can choose your friends but you can't choose your family. But even if you could, I'd never find one better than the one I already have. My mother and father's work ethic was ingrained in me from an early age and ensured I was never out of pocket or left wanting for anything. Despite my failings later in life, my mother always saw the best in me. She was the driving force behind my application to join the guards and was delighted when I joined the force. Without her, there would probably be nothing to write.

My sisters, Eileen and Maureen, and brothers, Myles, Philip and Noel, have provided me with life-long support and I'd like to thank them for encouraging me to write this book and for helping me in any way they could over the years. Although I was probably the apple of my mother's eye, *I* knew there were better pickings in the family tree.

When I married Susan Donohoe I doubled my luck and in the Donohoes I acquired another great family. And together we have two terrific sons in Thomas and Philip.

Thanks also to my (slightly) older relations – the Laverys and Shanahans in County Limerick – for their assistance piecing together some of my parents' early days, and Kathy Kelly in New York for her continued support.

Everybody needs good neighbours, or so the song goes,

and we couldn't have asked for better when we moved into Pearse Park. The Begadons and the Cunninghams made us feel welcome while Bernie Dwyer was like a sister to my mother and still serves a mean cup of tea whenever I call in.

Thanks to the Deise people, especially the Doyles, the 'Drumboe' Flynns and Tessie Power and her family for treating me like family any time I return to my home town, and also to Nancy, Beryl and Luke Hennessy for all the hot dinners and warm welcomes.

My time in the gardaí saw me meet some great people and make good friends. I worked under some fine officers such as Pat Byrne, Mick Carolan, Mick Carroll, Noel Conroy, John Courtney, Mick Finnegan, Tony Hickey, Tony McNamara and Fachtna Murphy.

To the older members of the Technical Bureau such as Pat Ennis, Earl Maher, Mick Niland and Andy Sharkey (who suffered serious injury in an explosion at the bureau during my time there), thanks for your guidance and help.

Thanks especially to Brendan Duffy and Declan Schutte for their loyalty on the job and their continued friendship, support and encouragement off it.

The diving instructors for the original Garda Sub-Aqua Unit had their work cut out for them but to Brian 'never-blow-your-fenzy-coming-into-a-bend' Cusack, John 'the-captain-of-the-ship' Hales and Seán 'someone-threw-me-knickers-in-the-water' Sheridan, I hope I didn't let you down.

Donal Gibbons's decision not to dive in the treacherous conditions off Whiddy Island should have been a lesson to me as a young garda, but I was always too quick to say yes.

To all the current members of the Garda Síochána, and indeed to anyone involved in such a high-pressure job, try not to get sucked in. Don't put yourself in danger and never put the job before your family.

The people of Ballyconnell made me feel like a local when I was sent on my first posting to the garda station there and in later years Seán Quinn and his staff at the Slieve Russell Hotel always looked after members of the Sub-Aqua Unit whenever we were called to searches in the area.

The Irish fishing fraternity, which has suffered many losses over the years, and indeed the families of every missing person I have come in contact with, are always in my mind. Together we will keep fighting the fight, keep searching for answers and hopefully one day we will all find peace.

Volunteer services – like the Boyne Fishermen's Rescue and Recovery and my colleagues in Searching for the Missing – are invaluable and never get the praise, support or funding that they should. Without these volunteers there would be a lot more people missing in Ireland.

Gerry Daly, whose son's remains were found in Oristown Bog, County Meath, in September 2014, after Gerry Junior had been missing for over three years, is an inspiration to those still searching for answers. Gerry Senior's remarkable ability to come to terms with the terrible tragedy that had hit his family – once his son's body was found – shows the vital importance of finding the missing. Until a loved one's remains are returned it can be impossible to make any sense of loss.

To my sober friends in AA, especially Gerry, thanks for your help and unwavering support over the past twenty-seven years and to the suffering alcoholics out there, all you need to do is surrender. Come to a meeting and ask for help. Help really is just around the corner when you put down that glass.

When I took up cycling I was lucky to join one of the best clubs in the country and regard Philip Cassidy and Brian Connaughton not only as mentors but as good friends to this day, while Peter Collins, Gerry Francis, George Ryan and Noel Tonge are always nearby. Thanks also to Edwin McGinn in England.

Thanks to Gay Farnan and Paddy Fitz for your support with the Missing People and to the members of the Irish Veteran Cyclists' Association for keeping the 'health farm' going.

In his own words, the late Seamus Kennedy taught me 'too much' on the bike. But watching 'Kenno' enjoy the sport at the highest level, while treating everyone involved with respect and courtesy, taught me a much bigger lesson off it and his kindness and generosity lives on in my memory.

In an effort to emulate 'Kenno' in some small way, and pass on my own knowledge of the sport, I now have three young cycling 'protégés' in Patrick, Richie and Seamus. Thanks for listening, lads, and for keeping me young.

Thanks to Gerard Cromwell for pulling this book together from hours and hours of interviews, stories, anecdotes and ramblings and to Sinéad, Aoife, Jack and Katie for allowing him the time to do so.

## ACKNOWLEDGEMENTS

Thanks to Faith O'Grady for living up to her name and having faith in the project from the start and to all at Penguin Ireland, especially Patricia Deevy, for keeping the reins tight whenever I veered off on a tangent.

Last, but not least, thanks to Noleen, for your kindness, understanding and patience.